Keeping It Personal

*Daily Wisdom
for Today's Woman*

Keeping It Personal

Daily Wisdom
for Today's Woman

JOAN HORNER

Premier Designs
INC.

Irving, Texas

*This book is dedicated
to my beloved husband, Andy,
whose love—and gentle pushing—
made this book idea become a reality;*

*to my children and grandchildren,
the joy of my heart;*

*and to my Premier family,
whom it is a joy to serve.*

Acknowledgments

My heartfelt thanks goes to:

Mary Horner Collins, the managing editor, and Eric and Elisa Stanford, who ably assisted in compiling this book.

Renee Blair, Nancy Grisham, Donna Horner, Jolie Horner, Kathryn Horner, Melanie Johnson, Barbara Lewis, and Sarah Wetzel for help with typing and preparing the manuscript.

Debbie Walton, Bill Wisdom, Ted Dysart, Martha Grammar, and Jeff DiMiceli in Premier's Creative and Events Services Department, for coordinating all the design and production details.

This "labor of love" would not have been completed without y'all.

Before You Begin . . .

If you spend any time at all around the Premier Designs crowd, one thing's for sure: you'll laugh, learn to accessorize, you'll get to know—I mean really know—great jewelry, you'll make friends, build a terrific business, and have a hands-down, slam-dunk ball. But why am I telling you this? You know better than I that the Premier Designs family is, well . . . a family.

And like any family, you feel loved and cared for. It's the culture of the company. I should know. My husband Ken and I, along with the ministry we help lead at Joni and Friends, are happy recipients of that love. We may not be Premier Jewelers like you, but Andy and Joan Horner have nevertheless wrapped their arms around us, encouraged us more times than we can count, and have often welcomed us into their home.

I'll never forget the time I led a Hymn-Sing in the spacious foyer of their beautiful house. There I was in my wheelchair facing their children and grandchildren who were sitting on the steps of the staircase. Joan and Andy were snuggled in between their grandkids, singing at the top of their lungs. Our harmony was so happy and heart-pumping, I thought, *This may be the Horner's vestibule, but it feels like the vestibule of heaven.* God really lives in their home!

A lot of people talk about God, but when you're with the Horners, you get the feeling they truly spend time with Him. You sense they know the Lord of the Universe on a first-name basis. Actually, they do. And it shows. You hear God's joy in their laughter, and you feel God's comfort with every hug. Consider this biblical description of what godly love looks like and tell me if it doesn't sound like them:

Love cares more for others than for self. Love doesn't want what it doesn't have. Love doesn't strut, doesn't have a swelled head, doesn't force itself on others, isn't always "me first," doesn't fly off the handle, doesn't keep score of the sins of others, doesn't revel when others grovel, takes pleasure in the flowering of truth, puts up with anything, trusts God always, always looks for the best, never looks back, but keeps going to the end. Love never gives up.
(1 Corinthians 13:4-7, THE MESSAGE)

Andy and Joan are always looking for ways to pass on this extraordinary and wonderful love of God. This is why I'm so glad Joan has written *Keeping It Personal: Daily Wisdom for Today's Woman*. This exceptional lady takes God very personally, so it doesn't surprise me that she delights in passing on His wisdom to you. After all, you are one of her Premier Jewelers; she cares about your soul, that deep innermost part of your being that aches for acceptance and longs to find peace and meaning in life.

You are holding in your hands a precious book that will not only help you find peace and real joy, but will show you how you can know this same God that Joan and Andy profess. Believe me, it's worth anything to be His friend. I've lived as a spinal-cord-injured quadriplegic in a wheelchair for forty years and I can tell you I'd rather be in my chair knowing Him, than be on my feet without Him.

I hope you will carve a little time out each day to "keep it personal" with Joan Horner. Brew a cup of coffee, find a comfy chair, and savor each inspirational daily vignette. When you do, you'll discover the source of her wisdom—the God of the Bible who desires to be personal with you.

Joni Eareckson Tada
Joni and Friends International Disability Center
Agoura, California

A Word from Andy Horner

In these days of great progress in technology, communicating is faster and easier but not necessarily better. We live in a time when we can talk to gadgets instead of people, and look at all the time it saves! In the midst of that, a company called Premier Designs was founded, a company that focuses on a Philosophy, Purpose, and Plan that is all about people.

Joan's passion from day one has been to keep our business "personal." This emphasis gives Premier Designs a warmth and caring attitude that technology can never offer. I am so glad someone has realized that life is much more joyful when we relate to each other more personally. It conveys a message that each person is important and helps them know they are "somebody special." The longer I live, the more I realize how vital it is to keep this personal touch.

Joan has practiced keeping it personal all her life. I, with thousands of others, am happy to know her passion remains strong today. May we all remember to "keep it personal."

With love always,
Andy

Introduction

I think the first person who encouraged me to compile some of my talks into a book was Randy Draper. Since that time, other folks have encouraged me to "put all that stuff in a book," and my husband, Andy, also got on the bandwagon. So we decided this was the time to put something together.

My mission in life is very simple: to keep it personal! That's also my mission for the Premier Designs family. So much of modern living is high tech and high speed, yet our culture is lacking in the social graces and relational touches. The corporate world is high tech too, with the end goal of making a profit as fast as you can and as efficiently as you can. If it saves money to have a machine answer the phone rather than a person, then the end (profit) justifies the means (impersonal with no service). Premier Designs' purpose is to influence people's lives, not just their pocketbooks, and to build relationships.

Premier Designs has a unique business culture. There are several reasons for that. One reason is that our desire is to honor God in all we do. Another reason for the difference between Premier and other companies is that our express purpose is "to enrich lives and serve others." That is the real personal touch. People are always more important than profits. People are our greatest asset!

I have compiled this book with that personal focus in mind. Most of these daily readings are taken from various presentations I have made over the years to different leadership groups, and at our national and regional rallies. You'll also find personal stories and anecdotes, as well as ideas that will help you grow your Premier business. I hope there is something for everyone: wisdom for your business life, encouragement for your personal relationships and family life, and truth from God's Word for your spiritual life.

I do not expect everyone to believe as I do, but I do want you to know my personal beliefs, which of course flavor this book. Because I am a Christian and love the Lord, this book freely uses stories, themes, and verses from the Bible. I believe the Bible is God's Word and offers us a wealth of truth and wisdom for living. I also believe that God is a loving and personal God, and wants to have a relationship with each of us through His Son, Jesus Christ. No matter what your religious perspective may be, I hope you can glean some helpful jewels of insight for your life here.

I pray that this book will challenge and inspire you to consider what "keeping it personal" really means for your business and your relationships. You'll be rewarded a thousand times over with the deep joy that only comes from giving and serving with that personal touch. May God bless you—personally!

Counting it all joy,
Joan Horner

January

This new year, look ahead
and strive to add something
positive to each life you
come in contact with,
expecting nothing in return.

With love,
Joan

January 1

A New Beginning

Great is his faithfulness; his mercies begin afresh each day.
Lamentations 3:23

A new year means new beginnings. I love Lamentations 3:23, which tells us that God's mercies "begin afresh each day." Grace and mercy new every day! Isn't that a great promise?

In this new year, what about your promises? Have you resolved to lose weight? Spend more time reading the Bible? Have dinner together more often as a family? Pray for your spouse every day? Be a friend to someone who needs one?

And what are your resolutions in your business? This is the time to move away from the ordinary. Now is the time to turn up more prospects, share more, manage people better, and get more done. Can you dream about that?

Dreaming can be threatening for some, but I trust that for you it will be exciting—a challenge to move onward and upward, a commitment to build your business, making it stronger in this new year.

The past year is gone, fading into history. Let's look forward, reaching beyond our dreams into the lives of those we encounter. How exciting to be reminded that God's mercies "begin afresh each day"!

Making It Personal

What new dream can I make a reality this year?

Strain toward the Future

*I am focusing all my energies on this one thing: Forgetting the past
and looking forward to what lies ahead, I strain to reach
the end of the race and receive the prize.*
Philippians 3:13-14

One thing I love about these verses in Philippians 3 is when the author, the apostle Paul, says very confidently that he is forgetting what is behind and *straining* toward what is ahead. Can you feel that? He's not just wishing and hoping to make it to the end of the race. He's not just ambling toward the prize. He's straining with all he's got. That means perseverance and grunt work—work, work, and more work!

Paul has given us excellent advice here, hasn't he? As this new year begins, keep looking toward and working for what is still ahead! Forget the disappointments, the postponements, the no-shows, the cancelled bookings. Forget the past, and strain ahead to those goals you want to reach.

Making It Personal

What things in the past are keeping me from moving ahead?

Personal Service

Greet each other in Christian love.
Romans 16:16

My real passion for our business is to impact our culture for good. One way to do that is by keeping it personal.

I was mentored by Mary Crowley, a very special woman who was the president of the Home Interiors and Gifts company. She always strove to keep that personal touch in her business. One way she did this was to sign thousands of commission checks by hand every month. I can remember the personal impact that had on people who received the checks.

From the very beginning I have wanted that same personal touch in Premier. Our business is all about people, and so many people are missing out on love, encouragement, and emotional support. We don't want our customers to call and be asked to "punch one, then punch two." All our phones are answered by a real person who says, "Good morning, Premier Designs. This is Bobbie. How may I serve you?" Between departments within the office, they are all trained to answer in the same way. If it takes twenty-four receptionists, we will always have a cheery personal answer when you call Premier Designs. That's one way to keep it personal.

Making It Personal

How can I keep a personal touch in my business?

The Foundation Is Vital

*Hear, O Israel! The L*ORD* is our God, the L*ORD* alone.*
Deuteronomy 6:4

This verse begins the celebrated Hebrew Shema, a Jewish prayer found in Deuteronomy 6:4-9. The truth upon which the nation of Israel was founded is: "The Lord is one God, the only God, and He is our God." Moses, the probable author of this book, knew how important it was to remember the foundational truths that made them a unique people.

The same is true for our company. Here are the foundational beliefs that make our company unique.

This is the Philosophy of our business:
- God created every person with value.
- Life's priorities should be God, family, and then career.
- We believe in America and the free enterprise system.
- People are our most important asset.

This is the Purpose of our business:
- To honor God in all we do.
- To enrich every life we touch.
- To provide a way to find identity, achievement, and success.
- To meet the personal and financial needs of our people.

Remember these business foundations and you'll build a solid business.

Making It Personal

What is the foundational philosophy that drives my business? My life?

January 5

The Strength of an Eagle

But those who wait on the LORD will find new strength.
They will fly high on wings like eagles.
Isaiah 40:31 *(Verse of the Year 2000)*

For centuries, the eagle has been admired for its great size and awesome power. That awesome bird can fly 150 miles per hour. Wow! When an eagle finds food, it folds its wings and dives at speeds up to 200 miles per hour. The eagle can soar to a height of half a mile.

An eagle's wings are very powerful and can carry objects almost as heavy as it is: about twelve pounds. The secret to its wings is that they are separate at the tips—like fingers on a hand. Because of the separation, many small whirlpools of air are formed instead of one large one. As the spinning currents expand, they collide, and this enables the eagle to fly indefinitely. It flaps its wings only on take off and during acceleration. The rest of the time it soars.

And the Bible tells us that those who trust in the Lord will mount up on wings like eagles! What a powerful image God uses.

Are you looking for new strength? Renew your trust in God. He will give you the strength of an eagle!

Making It Personal

What specifically can I do to trust in the Lord today?

Sense of Mission

In the same way, let your good deeds shine out for all to see,
so that everyone will praise your heavenly Father.
Matthew 5:16 (Verse of the Year 2002)

Most successful businesses have a clear sense of mission and purpose. They know what they are all about. Many times companies have a mission statement printed and hung in the reception area for all to see.

I believe that is a good model for each of us, in life and in our businesses. William James said, "The greatest use of a life is to spend it for something that will outlast it." Isn't that powerful?

Think about creating your own mission statement. Ask yourself: What do I want to invest in that will outlast me? Why has God put me here? What am I gifted to do? A personal mission statement helps us focus our efforts, and gives us freedom to say yes to the right things and no to other things.

Jesus said, "Let your light so shine before men, that they may see your good works and glorify your Father in heaven" (Matthew 5:16 NKJV). If you're looking for one, that verse would be a great mission statement. It certainly helps me to focus on a purpose that is eternal.

Making It Personal

Take some time to think about the questions above. Then write
out a simple mission statement for your life.

Doorway to the Heart

Look! Here I stand at the door and knock.
If you hear me calling and open the door, I will come in.
Revelation 3:20

A doorway is an entering place, an opening. Think about all the doorways we encounter in our everyday life. The door to school—and the education available there. The door to the dentist's office—and relief from a toothache. The door to the grocery store—to buy food so we can be healthy. The door to the church—where I began my walk with the Lord in 1951.

All of these doors are important, but the most important of all is the door to your heart. Have you ever thought of it that way? Imagine that the Lord Jesus is standing there. Jesus is there waiting, looking for you, because He loves you so much.

If you haven't already done so, maybe this will be the year to open the door of your heart and let Christ into your life. That's one doorway to lasting joy you don't want to miss.

Making It Personal

Am I ready to open the door of my life to Jesus?

S.E.R.V.E.

*For our people must learn to help all who need
their assistance, that their lives will be fruitful.*
Titus 3:14 (TLB) *(Verse of the Year 1994)*

We know it's good to help others, but how do we do it? Here is an acrostic with some suggestions:

Be **S**ensitive to other people's needs.

  Encourage others with our words and actions.

  Recognize people's accomplishments.

  Value our friends and coworkers.

  Enthusiastically offer to help.

It takes patience to be sensitive to a person's real needs. It takes time to encourage others. It takes humility to recognize and value another person's accomplishments, and it takes a lot of energy to help someone when you don't feel like it.

It may take sacrifice to do these things, but you'll never regret improving your S.E.R.V.E.

Making It Personal

Who is one person I can happily serve today?

Sharing Joy

There I will go to the altar of God, to God—the source of all my joy.
Psalm 43:4

What is the purpose of your life? Is it to honor God and serve others? Is it to enrich the lives of all you meet? If it is, then you are called to serve, care, and share. You are called to remind others of true joy! Strive to add something positive to each life you come in contact with, expecting nothing in return.

We can share joy with others because God gives joy to us. In Psalm 43:4 we read that God is the source of all joy. As we serve our heavenly Father, we will realize our hopes, our joy, and our very life all are dependent on Him. He is in control of our lives and our work, and we can leave the results to God.

Making It Personal

Who can I share joy with, expecting nothing in return?

Before You Speak

For from the heart come evil thoughts, . . . lying, and slander.
Matthew 15:19

There's a sickness going around. Most of us have it once in a while. It can be contagious and it can be harmful. I call it tongue-itis. We all struggle with taming our tongues. Here are some guidelines to help curb tongue-itis.

1. Before you speak ask yourself, *Is it necessary?*

2. Before you speak ask yourself, *Is it true?* Gossip is ugly. Don't participate in it. Don't pass on rumors. If what you want to say is not kind and helpful, then do not say it.

3. Before you speak ask yourself, *Am I a part of the solution or am I adding to the problem?* If you are not helping, then keep quiet.

Remember this: What is in the well of the heart comes up in the bucket of speech.

Making It Personal

What does my speech reveal about my heart?

Greatest of These

*There are three things that will endure—faith, hope, and love—
and the greatest of these is love.*
1 Corinthians 13:13

The loveliest description of love ever written is found in the Bible. Take some time to read the whole chapter of 1 Corinthians 13, and note all the actions involved in love.

> Love is patient and kind.
> Love is not jealous or boastful or proud or rude.
> Love does not demand its own way.
> Love is not irritable.
> Love does not keep a record of when it has
>   been wronged.
> Love is never glad about injustice.
> Love rejoices whenever the truth wins out.
> Love never gives up.
> Love never loses faith.
> Love is always hopeful.
> Love endures through every circumstance.
> Love will last forever.

What powerful words. This is not like any human love I've ever known. This is a God-kind of love, unconditional, strong, grace-filled, eternal. With God's help, we can learn to love like He does.

Making It Personal

*Who is the most loving person I know? What do I
admire most about her or him?*

Confident Expectation

"For I know the plans I have for you," says the LORD. "They are plans for good and not for disaster, to give you a future and a hope."
Jeremiah 29:11 (Verse of the Year 1998)

To hope means to have confident expectation. We don't hope for something and all the while think we won't get it. No, if we hope for it we expect it.

We begin hoping at a very early age. We hope we can stop at the ice cream stand on the way home from grocery shopping with mother. We are confident and expectant.

As I looked for the definition of the word *hope*, I found the term *hope chest* nearby, which was defined: "A chest used by a young woman for collecting clothing, linens and other personal articles in anticipation of marriage." That's confident expectation! That is true hope.

Whatever stage of life we are in, we can confidently expect God's provision for us. What is in your hope chest for the future?

Making It Personal

What are my biggest hopes? Do I have a confident expectation that they will be fulfilled?

Do What Is Right

"Are you really my son Esau?" [Isaac] asked. "Yes, of course," Jacob replied.
Genesis 27:24

Let's look at the life of a man named Jacob. Jacob's life was touched by God when he was young. He was the clear favorite of his mother. He had trouble with his twin sibling, which is not surprising. Jacob's name meant "deceiver," and he spent most of his 130 years doing his own thing.

This selfish trend began when Jacob saw the opportunity to get the coveted birthright from his brother Esau. He deceived his father to get his blessing (see Genesis 25:30-33; 27). "Oh what a tangled web we weave when first we practice to deceive," Sir Walter Scott wrote. Jacob's early deception led to countless problems in his life later on. His treachery affected his entire family, and at one point Jacob had to run for his life.

Our guiding slogan from the early days in our company has been: WIR/WBP—What Is Right and What Is Best for Premier. It is so easy to let little things slide. One small deception leads to another, doesn't it? Don't deceive, even in small things. Be honest and ethical. Be an example of integrity. You'll never be sorry.

Making It Personal

Am I committed to doing what is right?

The Wrestler

"Your name will no longer be Jacob," the man told him. "It is now Israel, because you have struggled with both God and men and have won."
Genesis 32:28

There are many lessons we can learn from Jacob's life. Jacob had gotten away with things so long that he didn't realize that God is a Judge. But God didn't stop working with Jacob. One night while Jacob camped alone, a man came and wrestled with him until dawn. When the man saw that he could not win the match, he struck Jacob's thigh and knocked it out of joint at the socket. Then the man said, "Let me go," but Jacob would not let go until the man blessed him.

Before the wrestling match, Jacob had come to the end of his own strength. He thought he was a dead man, for sure. He begged the Lord to rescue him from his brother Esau. When his thigh muscle was touched, Jacob became weak and humble. Jacob limped from that time on.

God touched Jacob at the very point where Jacob thought he was strongest. God changed his name from Jacob to Israel, meaning "one who struggles with God." God made him weaker, yet stronger as he depended on God.

Making It Personal

In what areas am I wrestling with God?

January 15

What a Change!

Then Jacob said to Joseph, "May . . . the God who has been my shepherd all my life . . . bless these boys."
Genesis 48:15-16

Jacob's wrestling match with God was the beginning of a new life for him. I remember vividly when my "new life" began.

I was twenty-four years old. I didn't have a wrestling match with God, but I was under conviction that I was not right with God. When I understood that my sin and rebellion separated me from God, then I put my trust in Jesus Christ. He is the One who died for my sin and made a way for me to know God.

My life changed completely that day. Just ask Andy. I didn't suddenly live a perfect life, but I did want to serve the Lord. I wanted Him to be in control of my life. I wanted to be a blessing to my little girl and a blessing to my friends.

After he wrestled with God, Jacob was different, too. When his son Joseph brought his sons for their grandfather's blessing, Jacob gave him an amazing blessing from God. That was something he could never have done in his old age if God hadn't touched him while he was young. I want to live a life of hope and blessing for my children and grandchildren. I want to make a difference. Don't you?

Making It Personal

How can I be a blessing to someone today?

Lead by Serving

[Jesus said,] "Whoever wants to be a leader among you must be your servant."
Mark 10:43

According to Jesus' words, a true leader is a servant. That sounds backwards doesn't it? But Jesus' life backed up the strength of His words. He showed us that:

- A servant leader will make the sacrifices that are needed.
- A servant leader will put others first and make them feel important.
- A servant leader will always try to lift up others in encouraging ways.
- A servant leader will be available.
- A servant leader will have a clear idea of where he or she is going and will pass on that vision.

Look at Jesus' life and test His words for yourself, and see if they're not true. Whoever wants to lead must serve.

Making It Personal

How does this concept of leading by serving differ from most leadership training?

Balancing Act

*[God] will give you all you need from day to day if you live for him
and make the Kingdom of God your primary concern.*
Matthew 6:33

When you are working full-time, keeping a healthy balance in your life is a tough challenge. I know because I have that same difficulty. Knowing your priorities helps you stay balanced.

The Bible is clear that God is to be first in our lives. That doesn't mean we go to church every day. It does mean that we are to consciously live for God's glory and be aware of God's presence every moment.

Whether you are married or unmarried, the second priority is your family relationships. Pray about your commitment to your family and be faithful in those areas.

Number three on the list of priorities is your business. This is the sticky part, isn't it? How much time do I spend on my job? What hours? What days? Map out a plan for your schedule so that you can utilize your time to a maximum.

Let your priorities lead the way in your decisions and schedule, and you will slowly become more balanced and blessed. What a relief to live with clear priorities!

Making It Personal

*What are my priorities? What steps can I take
to have a better balance in my life?*

Working Together

*Then make me truly happy by agreeing wholeheartedly with each other,
loving one another, and working together with one heart and purpose.*
Philippians 2:2

One thing that I'd love to see is the exciting Iditarod Trail sled dog race. Now the last time I checked, they don't run that race in sunny Florida. It's in snowy, cold Alaska. Since I don't like cold weather, I probably won't be watching that race in person anytime soon!

However, we did go to Alaska once and I found a wonderful print of the Iditarod. The sled team in that picture had nine dogs and one driver. The driver leads by giving instructions, pacing their run, steering them around any pitfalls in the road. He leads by his very presence in the sled.

Interesting concept, isn't it? They work as a team, but the driver is responsible for the final results. He prepares for the race ahead of time. He has the map. He knows the goal and makes plans to reach that goal. But selecting his team is crucial, because the team—especially that lead dog—is so very important.

Jim Miller, CEO of Miller Business Systems, once observed, "Coming together is a beginning, staying together is progress, and working together as a team is success." That is real teamwork.

Making It Personal

What team have I been on that worked well together? Why?

January 19

Teamwork Is an Attitude

So I run straight to the goal with purpose in every step.
1 Corinthians 9:26

For a team to reach a goal, they must believe in the power of teamwork. They must have the same commitment to the goal, and they must have people who will work together toward that goal.

Teamwork to me is a lot about attitude and a spirit of cooperation. You begin together, then you must nurture those on the team, and finally, you look for success. Teamwork can be destroyed quickly when one of the team has B.A.—bad attitude—or is not in sync.

Going back to the analogy of the Iditarod Trail sled dog race, picture one dog just loafing along, not caring at all about winning the race. That's all that is needed to change the attitude of the whole team. Or what if one dog got mad and headed home? The race would be lost.

A good attitude is so important to enable a team to stay with the plan and run straight to the goal. Then the purpose will be accomplished.

Making It Personal

Am I suffering from "B.A."? How can I be a better team member?

Wisdom for Business

Happy is the person who finds wisdom and gains understanding. For the profit of wisdom is better than silver, and her wages are better than gold. Wisdom is more precious than rubies; nothing you desire can compare with her.
Proverbs 3:13-15 (*Verse of the Year 1992*)

The book of Proverbs is a great manual for any businesswoman. In the first chapter, the author, King Solomon, clearly outlines the reason he compiled these sayings: "To teach people wisdom and discipline, and to help them understand wise sayings." If we pay attention to this book's principles, we'll receive instruction in discipline, good conduct, and in doing what is right, just, and fair.

Did you know that there are some verses in Proverbs written just for Premier Designs people? Listen to this: "For the profit of wisdom is better than silver, and her wages are better than gold. Wisdom is more precious than rubies; nothing you desire can compare with her" (Proverbs 3:14-15). (See, I told you—it's all about jewelry!) All joking aside, note how that verse ends. Nothing you desire can compare with wisdom. Nothing!

So pray now to desire wisdom, to grow in wisdom and discipline and understanding. Read the manual, Proverbs, and apply it to your business.

Making It Personal

How can the book of Proverbs help me in my business?

Time for Everything

*There is a time for everything, a season for every activity under heaven:
a time to be born and a time to die; a time to plant and a time to harvest.*
Ecclesiastes 3:1-2 (*Verse of the Year 1999*)

This wonderful passage was written by wise old King Solomon toward the end of his life. He had seen and done just about everything there was to see and do. He realized, "There is a time for everything."

The following anonymous poem reminds us that we have a choice about how we use our time.

*There's a time to get and a time to give;
a time to throw away.
There's a time to do a kindly deed,
and that time is today.
There's a time to sing and a time to mourn;
a time for joy and sorrow.
There's a time to love, but the time to hate
is better put off for tomorrow.
There's a time to sleep and a time to wake;
a time for work and play.
But the time to speak an encouraging word
is the time we have today.*

Making It Personal

**How does this truth about a time for
everything encourage me today?**

Will to Succeed

May he give you the desire of your heart and make all your plans succeed.
Psalm 20:4 (NIV)

What does it take to build a successful business? Hard work, disappointments, vision, goals, hard work, faith, training, a lot of determination, and more hard work.

What does it take to build a successful life? Hard work, disappointments, vision, goals, hard work, faith, determination…you get the idea. Success in any endeavor is like housework. It's never finished. It's sometimes messy and dirty. And you have to do it consistently, again and again. This is true in every area of your life. You must have:

- the WILL to achieve.
- the WILL to do your best.
- the WILL to overcome discouragement.
- the WILL to keep going.

Don't quit! Keep on! No one has it easy all the time. Stay with it when it's tough. Keep building and it will grow. And remember that you are not building alone. If you ask Him, God will strengthen you for the work of building a business—and a life.

Making It Personal

Looking at the list above, what areas of WILL do I need to work on in my business? In my life?

Faith Is the Foundation

It is impossible to please God without faith.
Hebrews 11:6

Many years ago we worked at Home Interiors and Gifts. My husband wrote the following words about that company as part of a tribute to Mary Crowley, the founder.

What do we have faith in?

1. *Faith in a God who is able.*
2. *Faith in the free enterprise system.*
3. *Faith in our country, America.*
4. *Faith in our company. When a policy comes out and you do not understand it, accept it and have faith it will be good for you.*
5. *Faith in people. We have the best customers, leaders, and people. You generally attract those who are like you.*
6. *Faith is the true foundation of our company. It begets trust and this trust develops relationships of harmony, which generate a sense of shared values.*

Those words written long ago are still a testimony of our belief system today. The Philosophy and Purpose upon which we founded Premier Designs hopefully will never change: to honor God, serve people, and enrich each life we touch. Methods may change, personalities will change, the product will change, but the foundation will remain the same.

Making It Personal
What do I have faith in?

The Highest Goal

I strain to reach the end of the race and receive the prize
for which God, through Christ Jesus, is calling us up to heaven.
Philippians 3:14

Going for the gold means going for the prize—first place. Did you ever wonder why gold became the symbol for first prize? Why isn't it silver or copper? One reason is that gold is the "king" of all metals. Gold can never be destroyed. Its form may change, but it is eternal in its beauty and use. A piece of gold jewelry today may possibly contain gold from the temple of Solomon or from an Egyptian tomb. Isn't that awesome?

Now the prize the apostle Paul is speaking of in Philippians 3:14 is greater than any gold prize. This prize is the highest award of all—to know Christ, to love Christ, to glorify Him! People often come to Andy for advice about their business. Countless times I have heard him say to those who are believers, "Your number one goal is to become like Christ, so that comes first before any other preparations you make." Before we set goals for our business, we must have the ultimate life goal in mind— that of knowing Christ.

Making It Personal

What is my number one goal? How can I
seek the higher prize of knowing Christ?

January 25

Pray First

O LORD, God of heaven, the great and awesome God who keeps his covenant of unfailing love … listen to my prayer!
Nehemiah 1:5-6

When we think of strong leaders, we find a good example in Nehemiah, a cupbearer to the king in ancient Persia. After years of living in exile in Persia, the Jewish people had been allowed to return to their homeland. But the walls of Jerusalem were in shambles, leaving it defenseless. When Nehemiah heard this, he knew he needed to go help.

There are many lessons to be learned from Nehemiah's experience. In the first chapter of the book of Nehemiah we find his secret: prayer. Nehemiah prayed and then courageously asked the king to allow him to return to Jerusalem to rebuild the city wall. The king agreed and even gave him letters of introduction to pave the way.

So I submit that the first step in becoming a good leader is to pray. Pray for courage, strength, and wisdom. Pray when you don't know what to do. Pray when you think you know what to do but need wisdom. Nehemiah eventually organized the rebuilding of the broken down walls of Jerusalem. And it all began with prayer.

Making It Personal

Do I see a need for prayer in my life?

Have a Plan

So I went up the Kidron Valley instead, inspecting the wall. . . . I said to them,
"Let us rebuild the wall of Jerusalem and rid ourselves of this disgrace!"
Nehemiah 2:15, 17-18

Have you ever started working on a craft or redecorating project before you really knew all the ins and outs, and then ended up with a pretty pathetic product? Sometimes we need to take a little time to assess our materials and read the instructions! Nehemiah was a leader who followed this planning-first principle.

Let's look at the story of Nehemiah again. As he led the people in building the walls of Jerusalem, he prayed first. But he did more than pray; he planned. He didn't start slapping mortar on the stones the day he got there. Before the work began, he made a careful survey of the walls. He wanted to assess the situation and know what was required. And it was a pretty big mess! Then, he called the people together and urged them to start the hard work. They divided the wall into sections, with different groups working on different parts, as their skills fit.

Nehemiah planned and prepared, prayed and worked, and all the while listened to the Lord. Next time you face a tough task, step back. Assess the situation. Be prayerful. Then make your plans.

Making It Personal

How can I plan more prayerfully?

January 27

Never Give Up

*Sanballat was very angry when he learned that we were rebuilding the wall,
. . . saying, "What does this bunch of poor, feeble Jews think they are doing?"*
Nehemiah 4:1-2

Nehemiah encouraged and inspired the people to rebuild the city walls, and they all got to work. And right away, what happened? There was criticism of the plan. "What do you think you're doing? There's no way you can do this!" his enemies mocked. (Read Nehemiah, chapter 4, for the details).

We all experience this at times. We might set a really important goal in our life or in our business, and a friend might say sweetly, "Oh, you'll never follow through." Or a spouse says, "Do you really think you can make money selling jewelry?"

Opposition seems inevitable. How did Nehemiah deal with it? He could handle criticism because he was looking to God. "We prayed to our God and guarded the city" (Nehemiah 4:9). God honored his prayers, his plan, and preparation, and in fifty-two days the work was finished.

Part of the unwritten job requirements for every leader is the ability to handle criticism. Nehemiah encountered repeated criticism, but his focus was steady and he never gave up. Develop your plans and then don't give up!

Making It Personal

How do I usually respond to criticism?

Always Honor Truth

They read from the Book of the Law of God and clearly explained the meaning of what was being read, helping the people understand each passage.
Nehemiah 8:8

You can spend hours building up a large group of people in your business, but if the inside core isn't functioning smoothly, the group will not grow and work effectively. Looking at Nehemiah's leadership example again, we see that he developed a common goal and focus for the people. Then he implemented an organizational structure to help the people accomplish the daunting task of rebuilding the city walls. He got the people grouped, protected, and relating smoothly with one another (see Nehemiah, chapters 3 and 4 for details).

How did Nehemiah do this? There were many ways, but one of his priorities was reading God's Word to the people. They were reminded of their common purpose. They listened to and honored the truth, and it made them stronger.

I am not saying you need to read the Bible at your meetings. Nehemiah was in a religious setting. But I am saying that you should honor the principles of God's Word. There are so few examples of truth and morality in business or government. Resolve to be a person who honors truth.

Making It Personal

*What difference would it make in my life if
I honored truth in all my relationships?*

January 29

The Word Brings Joy

So the people went away to eat and drink at a festive meal, to share gifts of food, and to celebrate with great joy because they had heard God's words.
Nehemiah 8:12

Settled back into their homeland after years of exile, the people gathered together to listen to the reading of the Book of the Law. They had not heard God's words for decades, and they stood for hours, paying close attention. Afterwards, they bowed down and worshiped, and many wept as the full import of what they heard hit their hearts. Nehemiah then urged them not to weep, but to celebrate God's goodness with food, gifts, and joy!

Did you get that? God's people heard God's Word, they were convicted by it, they repented and worshiped God, and then they had a party! I think many people associate the Bible, God's Word, with drudgery and rules and legalism. But really understanding God's Word always brings great joy.

Just what is joy? Is it excitement? Happiness? No, because excitement and happiness come and go. Joy is something that abides. We can't just wake up tomorrow morning and manufacture joy. Joy is of the Lord and from the Lord. It is a certainty and peace that comes from hearing God's Word and understanding it.

Making It Personal

**When was the last time I read the Bible?
How did I respond to what I read?**

No Ego Trips

Ezra the priest brought the scroll of the law before the assembly, which included the men and women and all the children old enough to understand.
Nehemiah 8:2

Nehemiah led the people in rebuilding the walls. But notice that he stepped aside to let Ezra do the job he was better qualified for, that of handling the Book of the Law. And while Ezra was reading the Scriptures, where was Nehemiah? He was standing among the people, listening to and learning from the same words and truths.

He could do this because he didn't care who received the credit. He wasn't trying to be everything to everybody. This was not an ego trip for him. He chose good men to help in the work. He used the strengths of others, and in so doing he developed their strengths more. Just think what an encouragement Nehemiah must have been to Ezra, and vice versa!

This is a great example for all leaders. Learn to be a follower at times, not always the big cheese.

Making It Personal

What do I learn from Nehemiah and Ezra's example?

Building a Business

The wall was finally finished. . . . When our enemies and the surrounding nations heard about it, they . . . realized that this work had been done with the help of our God.
Nehemiah 6:15-16

If you want some sound advice for building a business, just read through the book of Nehemiah. Let's review the principles we've gleaned from his example.

1. Pray about your business and about the people to whom God wants you to speak.
2. Be confident that your business is good for others.
3. Begin building your business. Be realistic about some opposition, but always trust God for success.
4. Teach and train your people diligently. They need to know the whys and hows so they can respond well.
5. Keep telling "your story." It will inspire people to pass it on!
6. Give God the glory. You cannot do it alone.

Making It Personal
Which of these insights would be most helpful to me right now in building my business?

February

Being a role model does
not make you a celebrity;
it makes you a servant,
with huge responsibilities.

With love,
Joan

Personal Touch

*If I could speak in any language in heaven or on earth
but didn't love others, I would only be making meaningless noise
like a loud gong or a clanging cymbal.*
1 Corinthians 13:1

Since day one my main thrust for the culture of our company has been to keep a personal touch in all our relationships and interactions. My mantra is: Keep it personal!

At our office all telephone calls are answered by a real person. Someone might say, "But it saves time to have voicemail." I say to them, "It's time well spent having a personal response, not an electronic one." That is keeping it personal.

We have tried desperately to know all our associates. It is a real sadness to us that we can no longer remember all the names of our growing staff, but there are still ways to relate on a personal level. That is keeping it personal.

We try to write handwritten notes to people. A computer-generated letter or certificate is fine, but a handwritten note makes it special. That is keeping it personal.

We have the opportunity to make a difference, person to person. I pray we can maintain that personal touch in all our relationships.

Making It Personal

What is one way I can relate to others in a more personal way?

How May I Serve You?

*Don't think only about your own affairs, but be interested
in others, too, and what they are doing. Your attitude should be
the same that Christ Jesus had.*
Philippians 2:4-5

The word *servant* conjures up images of an indentured slave who performs undesirable tasks, lacks self-esteem, and is often mistreated. But a real servant is someone who is secure and strong enough to humbly think of others more than herself or himself.

To me, service is an atmosphere involving everything we do and say. Service builds relationships with associates and customers. Real "success"—personally and professionally—comes from serving and caring.

The prevailing spirit in the world today seeks to be served, asking, "What are you going to do for me?" The biblical meaning of serving puts others first, and asks, "How may I serve you?"

Making It Personal

What keeps me from putting others before myself?

Power of Words

*We all make many mistakes, but those who control their tongues
can also control themselves in every other way.*
James 3:2

Many maxims have been written about the power of words, such as: "A long tongue means a short life" and "A sharp tongue is the only tool that grows sharper with constant use."

William Norris, an American journalist, wrote this little rhyme:

*If your lips would keep from slips
Five things observe with care—
To whom you speak, of whom you speak,
And how, and when, and where.*

Publius, the Greek sage, observed, "I have often regretted my speech, but never my silence." I heartily agree with him. Too often we just don't think before we speak. Next time you want to lash out with a quick verbal response—stop! Remember the power of words. Take a breath, count to ten, and then speak.

Making It Personal

How can I control my tongue today?

The Art of Modeling

*Be sure to do what you should, for then you will enjoy the personal
satisfaction of having done your work well…
For we are each responsible for our own conduct.*
Galatians 6:4-5

You may not realize it, but you are a role model. If you
are a parent, you are a role model. If you are a friend,
you are a role model. If you are a Premier Jeweler, you are a
role model. No matter what area of your life, you are most
likely influencing someone in some way.

We are all responsible for our own conduct. We cannot
blame anyone else when we react badly, treat others poorly,
or mess up. Nothing feels worse than doing what we know
is wrong and regretting it later. Being a role model can
sometimes be a scary thing, can't it?

But remember, being a role model does not mean
you have to be perfect. Being a role model also does not
make you a celebrity; it makes you a servant, with huge
responsibilities. "Be sure to do what you should," the Bible
tells us. Do your work well, and the role modeling will take
care of itself.

Making It Personal

How can I be a better role model for those around me?

Keeping Appearances

She dresses like royalty in gowns of finest cloth.
Proverbs 31:22

How do you make a statement about who you are without saying a word? By your personal appearance! My friend Mary Crowley used to say, "From the head up, we tell the world what we think of ourselves. From the shoulders down, the world will decide what they think of us!"

How we dress matters. We can dress to call attention to ourselves. We can dress to look fashionable or to impress someone. We can dress sloppily with no thought at all. No matter how we dress, it shows how we feel about other people and how we feel about ourselves.

I read about a teacher who talked to her high school students about the power of appearance. She asked, "When you see someone dressed like a policeman, what do you think that person does? If you saw someone walk into a bank with a stocking pulled over his head, what would you assume about that person? So what are you saying to people with the way you dress?"

What we wear is a statement to the people around us. It is an expression of who we are, and a message to the people we encounter. Be wise in how you dress.

Making It Personal

What impression am I making with my appearance?
What does it say about who I am?

Consistent and Calm

It was by faith that Moses' parents hid him for three months. ...
They were not afraid of what the king might do.
Hebrews 11:23

In the Old Testament book of Exodus we read of an extraordinary woman. Jochebed and her husband, Amram, lived as slaves in Egypt. Pharaoh ordered the execution of all Israelite baby boys at birth. Jochebed had a baby boy, but she and Amram hid him for three months. They were not afraid of the king. Why? "It was by faith."

What is faith? Hebrews 11:1-2 tells us, "It is the confident assurance that what we hope for is going to happen. It is the evidence of things we cannot yet see." Because of her faith, Jochebed was:

- consistent in her decisions. *(Am I consistent? Are my actions predictable?)*
- a woman with a calm spirit. *(What kind of spirit do I show my children? Does the whole household know it when I am upset?)*
- tireless. She refused to quit when facing overwhelming obstacles. *(Do I give up easily? How do I respond to situations beyond my control?)*

As a mother and grandmother I desire to be more consistent in my faith, calm in tough circumstances, and tireless in facing challenges.

Making It Personal

What can I learn from Jochebed's life?

Leadership 101

*Don't lord it over the people assigned to your care,
but lead them by your good example.*
1 Peter 5:3

Who was the greatest leader of all time? Winston Churchill? Napoleon? Eisenhower? One name stands out to me above all of them: Jesus Christ. Let's look at what we can learn from Jesus, the model leader. Some of these points are taken from *Leadership Lessons of Jesus*, written by Ray Pritchard, one of my favorite Bible teachers.

1. *A leader is called, and a leader calls followers.* "And a voice came from heaven saying, 'You are my beloved Son'" (Mark 1:11). Jesus was called by God, and then He called His disciples one at a time.
2. *A leader is a teacher.* "What sort of new teaching is this? . . . It has such authority!" (Mark 1:27). Jesus was the ultimate teacher.
3. *A leader serves.* "He took her by the hand and helped her to sit up, [and] the fever suddenly left" (Mark 1:31). Jesus served everyone he met with love and humility. It was not a weakness; but made him stronger.

There are countless other leadership lessons to learn from Jesus' life, but that's a start. Remember, good leaders have a vision. Better leaders share that vision. The *best* leaders invite others to join them.

Making It Personal

What is my calling? How am I called to lead?

Leadership 201

Rulers lead with my help, and nobles make righteous judgments.
Proverbs 8:16

L et's look further at the example of leadership Jesus gave us.

1. *Leaders eat with their people.* (I like this one!) "That night Levi invited Jesus and his disciples to be his dinner guests" (Mark 2:15). Meals were the backdrop for many of Jesus' lessons. Eating together is great for building relationships.

2. *Leaders will be criticized.* "At once the Pharisees went away…to discuss plans for killing Jesus" (Mark 3:6). If Jesus faced opposition, how much more will we? If you are a wise leader, you will understand there will always be those who oppose your leadership.

3. *Leaders win some and lose some.* "Some seed fell on shallow soil . . . and died. Still other seed fell on fertile soil and produced a crop" (Mark 4:5,8). Leaders who can't handle rejection usually don't last long. They must accept that some will catch the vision and some will not.

As we see from Jesus' life, being a leader requires commitment, flexibility, and sacrifice. But the rewards are great. Take a risk and practice leadership.

Making It Personal

What aspects of leadership do I fear?
How can I "lead" in better ways this week?

Real Wisdom

Fear of the LORD is the beginning of knowledge.
Only fools despise wisdom and discipline.
Proverbs 1:7

Proverbs is an ancient book of wise sayings mostly attributed to King Solomon. It is a practical book and has been called one of the best guidebooks to success ever written. Its purpose is to show us how to live with true wisdom. If you haven't done so, I encourage you to read through the book of Proverbs.

The book opens by saying that the fear of God is the beginning of all knowledge, or wisdom. To fear God means to reverence Him, stand in awe of Him. That is the first step in acquiring wisdom. The writer takes it a step further in Proverbs 13:10 and says, "Those who take advice are wise."

So how is your wisdom quotient? Are you fearing God or foolishly ignoring Him? Are you willing to take suggestions and advice, or foolishly think you know it all? Knowledge is knowing the facts but wisdom is using those facts. So get wisdom! Remember, real wisdom is "far more valuable than rubies" (Proverbs 8:11).

Making It Personal

What are some ways I can reverence and fear God today?

The Power of Influence

Dear friend, don't let this bad example influence you.
Follow only what is good.
3 John 1:11

Influence. We all have it, for good or for bad, as this story illustrates.

A lady bought a cockatoo bird. When she got the bird home and talked to it, the bird replied, "Let's kiss, let's kiss." After a few days, she tired of hearing only "Let's kiss." She called her pastor's wife, who also had a cockatoo. The pastor's wife suggested putting their birds together for awhile. "Maybe my bird's spirituality can rub off on yours." So they did just that.

As the lady listened in, her bird spoke first, "Let's kiss!" The spiritual bird said, "Let's pray." "Let's kiss…pray… kiss …pray." The birds kept this up for thirty minutes. *This is not working,* the woman thought. *I really hoped my bird would become more spiritual.* Later she heard her bird still saying, "Let's kiss." Then the other bird finally changed his tune and said, "My prayers are answered." Talk about influence!

The Bible says that one way to have a lasting influence is to have a generous heart and do good with what you have. Take your power of influence seriously and be an influencer for good.

Making It Personal

What kind of an influencer am I? Who am I influencing?

Daily Habits

You may say, "I am allowed to do anything." But I reply, "Not everything is good for you." And even though "I am allowed to do anything," I must not become a slave to anything.
1 Corinthians 6:12

Habits can be very positive or they can be very negative, but habits are always of great influence in our lives. Your habits can be major obstacles to becoming the kind of person you want to be. Virtually everything we do is the result of habit. Horace Mann described it well: "A habit is a cable; we weave a thread of it every day, and at last we cannot break it."

In the verse above, the apostle Paul speaks to this issue. He says if I want to habitually eat fried fast food, I can. But it is not good for me, so I must not become a slave to that. If I want to bite my nails down to the nub, it's legal to do that. But it is not good because I am a slave to it then. Some other habits that may enslave us might be cheating, overeating, or being negative. Procrastination can be a bad habit, stealing time, clouding motivation, and planting that word "LATER" in our hearts.

My mentor Mary Crowley often said: "In the beginning we make our habits, but in the end our habits make us." Our job is to form good habits and make them work for us.

Making It Personal
What habits do I need to break?

Be Honest

It is better to be poor and honest than rich and crooked.
Proverbs 28:6

There are so many ways of being dishonest. Lying and cheating are rather obvious. But it's also dishonest to tell half the truth, as this story illustrates.

Mrs. Johnson invited several friends to a mushroom steak dinner. When she opened the can of mushrooms, she noticed a film of scum on the top. She tested the mushrooms on her dog. He ate some and begged for more, so she felt they were safe. Dinner went well.

After dinner, the doorbell rang. Answering it, Mrs. Johnson saw her neighbor who announced briefly, "Mrs. Johnson, I'm so sorry, but your dog is laying out here dead." Then he left. Well, you can imagine the woman's consternation! She hurriedly called her doctor, who rushed over and pumped the stomachs of all her dinner guests. Then the doorbell rang. It was her neighbor again, "Mrs. Johnson, what do you want us to do with your dog's body? It's still on the side of the road where the car hit and killed him."

Mrs. Johnson's face went white. "Why didn't you tell me the whole story before?" she cried.

It may take more effort to tell the whole truth, but it's always the best policy.

Making It Personal

In what ways do I tell half-truths?

Don't Forget

Be very careful never to forget what you have seen the LORD do for you.
Do not let these things escape from your mind as long as you live!
Deuteronomy 4:9

In his novel *One Hundred Years of Solitude*, Gabriel Marquez tells the story of a little village that was afflicted by a strange plague of forgetfulness, a kind of contagious amnesia. This plague went through the population rather quickly, causing people to forget the name of even the most common objects. One young man, still unaffected, tried to limit the damage by putting labels on everything. "Table," "window," "dog." "Cow—milk every morning." Then at the entrance of the town, he put two signs. One read, "The name of our village is Macondo." The other sign read, "God exists!"

We are all forgetful sometimes. I believe some of this forgetfulness comes from the pace of the society in which we live. We are often overloaded, unfocused, and frazzled. We have that strange malady known as TMI—"Too Much Information." It is a fact that we will forget much of the information we have learned in life, such as how to do that math equation or our phone number when we were a child. Many things we forget really don't matter at all.

But we must never forget this: GOD EXISTS.

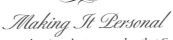

Making It Personal

What difference does it make to remember that God exists?

Loving People

*There are three things that will endure—faith, hope,
and love—and the greatest of these is love.*
1 Corinthians 13:13

Valentine's Day is observed to honor St. Valentine, a Christian martyr who died in Rome in A.D. 270. For more than five hundred years now, a valentine has been an expression of affection. It may be a card, a message, a gift, a piece of artwork, anything that expresses affection. Love is the theme.

We hear the world crying out, "I want to be loved." We all need encouragement. We all need to be loved. We all need to give love.

We often say that we "love those pearls" or we "love that jacket." Mary Crowley taught me that in reality we can only love people. "We *like* things, but we *love* people," she used to say, and I've never forgotten that.

This is a perfect time of year to review the objects of our love. Do we love pearls—and ignore our coworkers? Or do we love people and like things?

On Valentine's Day, my focus is to love more and to encourage more. It is in loving that we feel loved; it is in encouraging that we are encouraged.

Making It Personal

How can I show more love to the people in my life?

February 15

Defining Love

We know what real love is because Christ gave up his life for us.
1 John 3:16

I read about a sociology professor who gave her freshmen students an interesting assignment one year. Each student was to ask a random sample of at least thirty people to respond to the following:

1. Give your definition of love.
2. Name five actions that you consider to be acts of love.

Almost 1,500 people were interviewed—and no two gave the same answers. Amazing isn't it? I would venture to say that each of us would give a different definition of love as well.

We may find it difficult to define love, but God does have a definitive answer. He tells us that love is not primarily a feeling; it is a commitment. How did God say "I love you?" By giving us His one and only Son. That is commitment—that is love.

Making It Personal

How do I define love?

The Best Parent

You are citizens along with all of God's holy people.
You are members of God's family.
Ephesians 2:19

If you are a parent, you are familiar with the joys and challenges it can bring. Parents want what is best for their children. That does not always mean we give them everything they want. Each child's needs are different.

If we are in God's family, just think what it means to have God as our Parent!

1. God loves us with a perfect love.
2. God will never leave us.
3. God provides for our needs.

It was a painful, costly process for God the Father to make us His children. He gave His only Son to die for our sins. When we believe in Christ, we are sealed forever as His children. No one can ever pluck us from the Father's hands; nothing can separate us from His love. I have known this ever since I first believed.

We can find perfect love and perfect security with our perfect heavenly Parent.

Making It Personal

What do I appreciate about my parents?

Lavish Love

Now glory be to God! By his mighty power at work within us, he is able to accomplish infinitely more than we would ever dare to ask or hope.
Ephesians 3:20

I remember when our son Tommy was very little, he tended toward the naughty side and had to be punished regularly. Try as we might, we could not convince him that we did this because we loved him. If we didn't care, we would have let him go his reckless way. One day I bought him a small gift, just a little bag of marbles, and put it in his room with a note that told him again how much we loved him. Do you think he believed it then? Yes, he did . . . until the next time we had to discipline him.

My gift of marbles wasn't exactly lavish, but it is a tiny picture of how God is. He is lavish in His goodness. He shows us how much He loves us with all His gifts to us. He never gives up on us. He shows His love in countless ways, superabundantly. By His mighty power at work within us, He is able to accomplish infinitely more than we would ever dare to ask or hope.

Making It Personal

What lavish gift of God's love can I thank Him for today?

Do Re Mi

Get rid of all bitterness, rage, anger, harsh words, and slander. . . .
Instead, be kind to each other, tenderhearted, forgiving one another,
just as God through Christ has forgiven you.
EPHESIANS 4:31-32

I came across the following anonymous acronym using the words of the musical scale. See what nuggets of wisdom you can glean here, and then make music with them in your life.

DO— Do count your blessings before you count cares. Don't worry about things that may never happen.

RE — Radiate a joyful spirit. Like laughter, it is infectious and makes others feel better.

MI — Mete out kindness, understanding, tolerance, and forgiveness generously.

FA — Far-reaching are the benefits of spiritual thinking. You become as you habitually think. Resentment, hatred, and envy will gnaw on your spirit.

SO — Sow the seeds of love, friendship, empathy, and helpfulness.

LA — Laugh at yourself now and then. Someone who can laugh at herself is less apt to be at war with herself.

TI — Teach yourself to appreciate all the wonders of nature. Thank God daily for the precious gift of life.

DO — Do not expect someone else to open the door to happiness for you. You must do it yourself. It is a choice.

Making It Personal

Which notes do I want to "sing" today?

Never Too Young

Don't let anyone think less of you because you are young.
Be an example to all believers in what you teach,
in the way you live, in your love, your faith, and your purity.
1 Timothy 4:12

In the Bible, it is surprising how many people God called to do a special work when they were very young. Consider Samuel, called to serve God when he was probably only five or six years old. Moses was protected while he was a tiny baby. David was anointed as king when he was a teenager. Daniel was probably about twelve years of age when he was taken from his homeland into captivity.

In the verse above, the apostle Paul says we are not to think any less of a person because they are young. It is natural for us to equate youth with lack of experience or with lack of sincerity. But God warns against that. It is often easier for a young person to listen to God's voice, to really hear His calling, and then to obey with childlike faith.

I think one reason God calls a person when he or she is young is to give them the wonderful opportunity to really live a life of significance, one that will really count for eternity. It allows a person time to understand his or her purpose. Whether we follow God early or late in our lives, we can always live with love and faith and purity.

Making It Personal

What young people do I know who are an example of love and faith?

God Is at Work

And I am sure that God, who began the good work within you,
will continue his work until it is finally finished
on that day when Christ Jesus comes back again.
Philippians 1:6

This is a favorite verse of mine. "I am sure [confident] that God, who began the good work within you [in me], will continue his work until it is finally finished." Isn't that a great promise!

God will do the work, but that does not excuse us from being obedient to God's will. God is always trying to build our character and mold us into the people He wants us to be. And don't worry, God can and will do His good work in any person, no matter what your personality, education, or background.

In Jeremiah 1:5 God says, "I knew you before I formed you in your mother's womb. Before you were born I set you apart." Wow! That means before I was born in Woodstock, Canada, God knew me. Out of all the millions of people, God knew me! And He knows you, too. Trust Him to do a good work in your life.

Making It Personal

In what ways do I see God at work in my life?

Are You Listening?

What a shame, what folly, to give advice before listening to the facts!
Proverbs 18:13

Have you ever thought about what it requires to really listen to another person? *Webster's Dictionary* defines *listening* as "giving close attention in order to hear." Hearing and listening can be two different things.

There are two ways of hearing: (1) to perceive the sound, just hear the noise, and (2) to perceive the sound going past the ear into our hearts and minds. Most of us are so busy all the time that we don't really listen. We may hear the sounds, but it doesn't really enter our hearts.

If we can be quiet when someone is talking to us and look them in the eye, we are communicating, "You matter to me." Then we are really listening.

Making It Personal

Am I a good listener, or just a hearer?

The Cost of Being Lazy

We urge you to warn those who are lazy.
1 Thessalonians 5:14

These are some of the apostle Paul's last words of advice to the Christian church in the ancient city of Thessalonica. If we really listen to his words, not just hear but listen with our hearts, I believe we will be better servants and better leaders.

"Warn those who are lazy," he urges. There must have been a real problem if it warranted such an urgent warning. What is so bad about being lazy? The book of Proverbs helps us answer that question:

- Laziness can ruin you. "But you, lazybones, how long will you sleep?" (Proverbs 6:9)
- Laziness can make you poor. "Lazy people are soon poor; hard workers get rich." (Proverbs 10:4)
- Lazy people end up working for others. "Work hard and become a leader; be lazy and become a slave." (Proverbs 12:24)
- Lazy people make excuses. "The lazy person is full of excuses, saying, 'If I go outside, I might meet a lion in the street and be killed!' " (Proverbs 22:13)
- Lazy people oversleep. "As a door turns back and forth on its hinges, so the lazy person turns over in bed." (Proverbs 26:14)

Are you listening?

Making It Personal

How can I fight against laziness in my life? in my business?

February 23

Words for the Timid

*Encourage those who are timid. Take tender care of
those who are weak. Be patient with everyone.*
1 Thessalonians 5:14

Some of you do not relate at all to being timid or shy. You are just the opposite! But many of you have worked diligently to get out of your comfort zone of shyness. The writer Paul recognized that timid people are worthy of encouragement.

Many years ago I thought of myself as just a housewife. The work was so daily, so mundane, no glory in it at all. I was shy about doing other things. But then I realized that for a season, that was just what I *did*, not who I *was*, and there's a difference between the two. I am a child of God, and my confidence is in Him! Romans 12:3 (NIV) says, "Don't think of yourself more highly than you ought." But does that give us permission to think too lowly of ourselves? No, we are all God's workmanship, created in His image.

If you struggle with a lack of confidence and shyness in relationships, remember who you are and whose you are! If you are not timid, but know someone who is, take the time to tenderly encourage her.

Making It Personal

**Whether I'm shy or not, who can I encourage today
who might be struggling?**

Good Soil

He told many stories such as this one:
"A farmer went out to plant some seed."
Matthew 13:3

I read that 35 percent of all Jesus' teaching in the New Testament was done in parables. A parable is an earthly story with a heavenly meaning. Jesus was a master teacher but He did not reveal all truth. Rather, He chose to conceal certain truths in parables.

One of my favorites is the parable of the farmer and the soils found in Matthew 13. The farmer scattered his seed across a field, but he wasn't too successful. The birds ate some of it. Other seeds fell on rocky soil. They grew but quickly wilted because they had no nourishment in the shallow soil. Other seeds fell among thorns and were choked out. But some seeds fell on fertile soil and produced a crop yielding 30, 60, and 100 times increase.

The farmer didn't stop sowing seeds because of the birds and rocks and thorns. He knew there was good soil too, and that it would be worth it. Thank goodness God is like that with us. He doesn't give up on us until we, like fertile soil, can bear good fruit for His glory.

Making It Personal

If Jesus were scattering the seed of His love across the soil of my heart,
which type of soil would describe my response right now?

Premier Soil

But some seeds fell on fertile soil and produced a crop that was thirty, sixty, and even a hundred times as much as had been planted.
Matthew 13:8

Let's look again at Jesus' parable of the seed and soils and relate it to your business. Just as in the parable, there are three types of responses to beginning a business.

1. *Seeds on the rocky soil.* These seeds sprout quickly and burn out quickly. Some people begin their work with great enthusiasm. They are "shooting stars" as my husband Andy calls them. They may prosper quickly but then they fizzle out because they lack strong roots.

2. *Seeds among weeds and thorns.* This woman has a difficult time because of the constant "weeds" of negative criticism she gets. "You're wasting your time." "It's not going to work." "You don't have the personality for sales." Negative criticism has choked many good people with potential.

3. *Seeds on fertile ground.* This person realizes that her business requires hard work. She takes advantage of training and builds good relationships, which are like rain soaking into her fertile ground. She grows as a person, loves to learn, loves people, and loves to work.

Making It Personal

What are some rocks and weeds affecting my business right now?

The Power of a Name

*Choose a good reputation over great riches, for being held
in high esteem is better than having silver or gold.*
Proverbs 22:1 (Verse of the Year 2003)

How important is your name to you? When you are promoted and receive an award, what if we said, "Hey, you with the red polka dot skirt and orange striped jacket, come up here and we'll promote you." Would that excite you? Of course not. We all love to hear our names called out. Our names are significant and give us an identity that sets us apart.

People can associate good things or bad things with our name. As a child I never really liked my middle name, Vivian. There was a girl in my second-grade class named Vivian who always had dirty hair and filthy, ragged clothes. For some reason I always associated my name with her appearance and, sadly, that influenced how I viewed my name for a long time. What is your name associated with?

Our Premier company name is important too. The word *Premier* means "superior, best, first class." But it's not really the name that makes or breaks our business. It is the quality of the product and the integrity of our service that makes the name of Premier mean something. Proverbs 22:1 tells us to choose a good reputation—a good name—over riches. That's a lifelong goal.

Making It Personal

What does my name mean to me?

Honoring God's Name

Do not misuse the name of the LORD your God. The LORD
will not let you go unpunished if you misuse his name.
Exodus 20:7

When we hear God's name used in a casual or flippant way, it should concern us. We preface a hard-to-believe story with "Honest to God," trying to make it sound more truthful. "Oh God" and "My Lord" are used as meaningless exclamations. It really grieves me to hear it.

Over the years, the wording of various oaths was shortened and today, these "swearing" words are used frequently by people who do not realize what they are saying. Let me list a few of these traps:

"*Jesus*" is now "*gee whiz, jeez, gee, gee willikers.*"

"*Christ*" is now "*cripes, jiminy Christmas,*
   jeepers creepers."

"*God*" is now "*Gosh, golly.*"

Most people will say that they may use these words but don't mean anything by them. Maybe you think that. Well, that is just the point. We are a culture that uses God's name as though it had no meaning.

But God's name does have value and worth. His name is awesome. His name is above all other names. His name will endure forever. It's a serious thing to use His name irreverently.

Making It Personal

How do I treat God's name?

Planning for Success

Commit your work to the LORD, and then your plans will succeed.
Proverbs 16:3 (*Verse of the Year 1995*)

What are your plans? For your business maybe you have plans to:

- serve your colleagues and customers to the best of your ability.
- enrich lives—to encourage, be a friend, show appreciation, demonstrate that you care.
- have 100 Home Shows.
- become a leader.

In your life maybe you have plans to:

- raise good kids.
- take care of an elderly parent.
- volunteer in your community.
- teach a Bible study.

God will be involved in your plans if you invite Him to be. I believe God wants us to use our gifts and abilities to the maximum. None of us has all the talent and all the gifts. So when you plan, make use of other people's gifts and strengths. Work hard, plan well, and above all, commit your plans to God, and they will succeed.

Making It Personal

*What plans for my work or my life do I
need to think through this week?*

March

Take heart in this new season of spring. Ask God for wisdom to use the gifts He has given you, and believe that God will do great things!

With love,
Joan

Known for a Personal Touch

For God is not unfair. He will not forget how hard you have worked for him and how you have shown your love to him by caring for other[s].
Hebrews 6:10

Personal service is very hard to find, as you might have noticed. On the whole, our culture is becoming more socially fragmented as we spend more time in front of computer screens and less time developing relationships. At about the time our country changed from a manufacturing economy to a service economy, real service began to spiral downward.

Our company has a web site on the Internet and we depend upon computers to fulfill orders and serve our customers. Computers are good things. But we are to appreciate the computer as a tool, not a toy; a tool that we can control and not vice versa. We must find a way, even in the maze of technology, to add a dimension of personal involvement to our jobs—real people relating to real people.

And that is my commitment: to have a personal touch. I don't want Premier Designs to be known only for having the best jewelry (which it does), nor for having the most gorgeous catalog (which it does), but to be known for caring enough to have that personal touch.

Making It Personal

What does it mean to me to be treated with a personal touch? What would it take for me to treat someone else with a personal touch?

Giving Thanks for Everything

It is good to give thanks to the LORD. It is good to proclaim your unfailing love in the morning, your faithfulness in the evening.
Psalms 92:1-2

There are so many things for which to be thankful. In the morning we can thank God for another day, for good health, for giving us purpose and hope. In the evening we can thank God for new friends we have met, for His provision of food and shelter. But can we say thanks even when we experience poor health, a crisis with our teenager, or slow business this month?

"No matter what happens, always be thankful," the Bible says (1 Thessalonians 5:18). Why? Because this is God's will for those who follow Him. We are not thanking God *for* the bad events, but thanking Him *in* and *through* them. After all, God is in control of our lives, and He allows these tribulations for reasons only He knows. Because He is in control and He is good, then we can truly be thankful. We know that He is working His good purposes in our lives. Romans 8:28 tells us: "We know that God causes everything to work together for the good of those who love God and are called according to His purpose for them."

What makes us thankful? Knowing that God is in control and that He is loving and good.

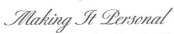

Making It Personal

Tonight, before you go to sleep, tell God how thankful you are for His love and faithfulness.

A Snapshot of Serving

*Care for the flock of God entrusted to you...not for what you will
get out of it, but because you are eager to serve God.*
1 Peter 5:2

If we were to take a picture of a person who serves, here are some images we might see:

- Someone who is a people-helper.
- Someone who doesn't look for reward or service in return.
- Someone who serves with joy.
- Someone who is others-absorbed.
- Someone who celebrates another's good fortune.
- Someone who is happy to help no matter what the cost.

If you give only to get, you're not really giving at all; you're just trading. The world doesn't need our merchandise; it needs our service.

Making It Personal

Am I willing to do whatever it takes to serve?

Like Sunshine!

Let the smile of your face shine on us, LORD.
Psalm 4:6

March is the last hurrah of winter, when flowers and their colors are hidden. But we are approaching the time of longer days and more sunshine. When spring showers hit, there is color in the garden again. The sun comes out, there is hope of new life and our spirits start to lift.

What sunshine is to flowers, smiles are to human beings. As Proverbs 15:13 tells us, "a glad heart makes a happy face." But a happy face can also make a glad heart. Genuine smiles show appreciation, love, and care.

We can all be like sunshine. We can all show that we care. We can all smile!

Making It Personal

Who needs to see my smile today?

Trickle-Down Joy

Always be full of joy in the Lord. I say it again—rejoice!
Philippians 4:4

Consider the Christian businessmen and businesswomen you know. Are they perfect? No, of course not. None of us is perfect. But when they are at their best—working well with people, serving others, acting with integrity—isn't there a special spirit about them? I think you will agree with me that there is. How do you explain this? I think I can sum it up in one word: joy.

Someone has said, "The spirit of a place trickles down from the top." And I might add, "and goes right through the organization." A spirit of joy comes through positive and focused people who are excited about what they are doing.

You may have heard Chuck Swindoll's famous quote, "Life is 10 percent what happens to you and 90 percent how you respond to that 10 percent." Whatever our circumstances are—that 10 percent of what happens to us—we can have the joy of the Lord. And that joy will spill over to others.

Making It Personal

Am I passing on joy to others?

Think Before You Speak

Blessing and cursing come pouring out of the same mouth.
Surely, my brothers and sisters, this is not right!
James 3:10

Norman Vincent Peale told a story about Branch Rickey, the head of the old Brooklyn Dodgers baseball team. The story goes like this.

Rickey was attending a meeting to negotiate a contract for pro football at Ebbetts Field. Suddenly, Rickey threw down his pencil, pushed back his chair, and growled, "The deal's off!" Surprised, the other men asked why, especially since they seemed to be close to a deal involving big money.

Mr. Rickey answered, staring right at one of the football representatives, "Because I don't like the way you've been talking about a friend of mine."

The football agent asked, "What friend? I haven't been talking about anyone, let alone a friend of yours."

"Oh, yes you have," Rickey answered. "You've mentioned Him in almost every sentence. You have repeatedly used the name of Jesus Christ in a profane way."

Most tongues are tied in the middle, wagging at both ends. The Bible says that with the same tongue we praise God and then curse men, but this isn't right. Honor God's name and honor others by thinking before you speak.

Making It Personal

What careless things do I say without thinking?

Put Your Name In

*Love is patient and kind. Love is not jealous or boastful or
proud or rude. Love does not demand its own way. Love is
not irritable, and it keeps no record of when it has been wronged.*
1 Corinthians 13:4-5 (*Verse of the Year 1987*)

Years ago I taught high-school sophomores in Sunday
school and loved it. One Sunday we were studying
1 Corinthians 13, and one of my favorite memories was
the day we put our own names in place of the word *love*:
"*Joan* is patient and kind; *Joan* is not irritable; *Joan* never
gives up." We all laughed, sighed, showed disappointment.
It wasn't too hard to see how short we fell of the standard
of real love.

Let's look at just one of these: "Joan is patient and
kind." Am I patient when I have to wait for two hours for
my doctor appointment? Am I patient with my colleagues
when we disagree? Am I patient when the service at a store
is awful? Well, okay, I need to just stop there with that first
line about love. If I were batting, I'd already be an early
strike-out victim!

How about you? Put your name in the whole list of
descriptions of love in 1 Corinthians 13. Are you patient
with your family? Kind with a colleague who won't follow
your coaching? Patient when there's a back order? Love is.

Making It Personal

**In what area of my life do I need to really
work on patience and kindness?**

Hope Deferred

*Hope deferred makes the heart sick, but
when dreams come true, there is life and joy.*
Proverbs 13:12 (*Verse of the Year 2006*)

Who of us has not been disappointed when our dreams and hopes have been drawn out in time? For instance, when we have been anticipating a vacation and it is put "on hold," we are heartsick, aren't we? That is hope deferred—delayed and drawn out.

I remember years ago when my husband's company moved us to Racine, Wisconsin. We left the nice warm temperatures of Dallas in March with the hope of living on the lake in Wisconsin. We arrived in Racine wearing summer clothes—and temperatures in the 30s greeted us. Where was the lovely spring weather? No flowers, no green grass, no green leaves on the trees. Only snow everywhere! My hopes were dashed. I was devastated. I found out quickly that I am a creature with feelings totally conditional on the weather! Hope was deferred until summer arrived, and with it, life and joy.

When our hopes are realized, our longings are fulfilled, our dreams have come true, we are no longer heartsick. We have life and joy—we are satisfied. We are renewed physically and spiritually. This is the hope God offers us!

Making It Personal
**When have I experienced a hope put "on hold,"
and then fulfilled later?**

Sweet Friendship

A friend loves at all times.
Proverbs 17:17 (NIV)

Friendship is an art. We all know the satisfaction and benefits of good friendships. There is a real security in having a good friend. We also know that people who seem to be friends sometimes betray us, hurt us, and disappoint us. They are not true friends in the end.

While our emphasis seems to be on *having* friends, the truth is that in order to have friends, we first must *be* a friend. And so we each need to learn the art of being a friend.

Proverbs 17:17 tells us, "A friend loves at all times." This means that a friend continues to love, and to show his or her love, whatever the circumstances. A friend is one who knows you and still loves you. A true friend helps you when your need is great.

Friendship is love expressed in acceptance of another person. It is consistent. It is being the one person someone else can count on.

Our business can be a wonderful way for women to learn the art of friendship. We can be a real help to others in time of need. We can accept people for who they are. We can be a consistent presence, an encourager, and a loyal adviser.

Making It Personal
How can I be the friend others would desire me to be?

The Power of One

So Hilkiah the priest . . . went to consult with the prophet Huldah.
2 Kings 22:14

The prophetess Huldah was highly regarded. During a time of despair and confusion, her words from God turned a whole nation around. An important lesson we learn from Huldah is the power and influence of *one person*. God can and will work through one woman.

I believe women are uniquely created by God for two purposes. One purpose is to be a partner and helpmate to a husband (if God so chooses to give her a husband). I also believe that God created women to have their own special influence in their world. I haven't always thought that way. When I was young, I thought that women were mostly meant to be a helpmate—living in the shadow of a man, so to speak. But when I became a Christian, my ideas changed. I realized how important it is to be a woman of influence.

Ephesians 2:10 says that "we are God's masterpiece. He has created us anew in Christ Jesus, so that we can do the good things he planned for us long ago." God has built into each of us unique talents and gifts. Don't ever underestimate the power of one person.

Making It Personal

How can I use my unique influence to encourage someone today?

Speak Out

[Huldah] said to them, "The LORD, the God of Israel, has spoken!
Go and tell the man who sent you, 'This is what the LORD says . . .'"
2 Kings 22:15-16

W hen King Josiah listened to what was written in the Book of the Law, he quickly realized they had not been doing what the Law said. They needed help. So Hilkiah the priest consulted with the prophetess Huldah.

Why Huldah? There were other knowledgeable prophets around. Yet, he sought out Huldah. Married to Shallum, the keeper of the Temple wardrobe, she was not a woman of means. All the same, she was no ordinary woman.

There are two great qualities we see in Huldah as we read between the lines: (1) She had a pure heart, which gave her the ability to use her prophetic insight wisely; and (2) she had power, because she loved God with all her heart. If you read the story for yourself, you'll note that she was careful to ensure that the king understood these were not her words, but the words of the Lord. And she wasn't afraid to speak out.

Each of us can be a channel to do good if we allow God to speak through us. We should not become infatuated with our own words. Like Huldah, we need to stay close to God to know when to speak and what to say.

Making It Personal

Is there a situation in my life today where I need to speak out?

Lead by Influence

*They give generously to those in need. Their good deeds will
never be forgotten. They will have influence and honor.*
Psalm 112:9

Being a leader is a solemn and serious calling. It may appear to be glamorous, but leadership is a tough job and is getting tougher every year. A leader works hard and often without thanks. It can be "lonely at the top."

There are dozens of definitions of leadership. I like how my husband, Andy, describes it: *Leadership is fulfilling the needs of those who follow.* In addition, I think leadership means one who has influence. Some of you will have more influence than others. But I believe we are all here to make a difference, and to enrich and influence the lives of those we touch.

The late President Harry Truman referred to leaders as "people who can get others to do what they don't want to do, and make them like doing it." That is real influence. That is being a real leader.

Making It Personal

How can I influence others for good and fulfill their needs?

Ask for Help

*"This is not good!" his father-in-law exclaimed. "You're
going to wear yourself out, and the people, too. This job is
too heavy a burden for you to handle all by yourself."*
Exodus 18:17-18

How do we balance family and business? How can we do everything we need to do every day? If you feel overwhelmed, it's time to call for help!

In the book of Exodus we read a story about Moses, the leader of the Israelites. At this time, Moses was completely out of balance, allowing his work to consume all his time. He was somewhat defensive, as most busy people are. "The people called me; they need me." He was trying to justify his too-busy schedule. But his father-in-law, Jethro, was not buying it. He wasn't impressed as he watched Moses run himself ragged, eating on the run, meeting deadlines, making decisions of all kinds.

Jethro reproved Moses strongly. In three words he solved the problem: *Call for help!* Then "you will be able to endure," Jethro said. In other words, Moses would be around for the long haul, not just a short flash.

Are you doing too much by yourself? Are you tired of feeling exhausted? We all need help to balance work, family, recreation, time alone, and time with others. Don't be afraid to ask for it.

Making It Personal

*Do I need help to make some changes and
to balance my life? Whom can I call?*

Team Harmony

> *May God, who gives this patience and encouragement,*
> *help you live in complete harmony with each other.*
> **Romans 15:5**

There is a story about a mother who hoped to inspire her nine-year-old son to practice piano more by taking him to see the great pianist Paderewski. As they waited for the concert to begin, the boy slipped away and went to look at the lovely concert grand piano. Suddenly, he jumped on the stage, sat on the stool, and began to play "Chopsticks." The audience was horrified: "Get that boy away from there! Somebody stop him!"

Backstage, the master pianist heard the commotion and rushed to the stage. Without one word, he stooped over behind the boy, reached around both sides, and began to improvise a counter-melody to harmonize with "Chopsticks." As the two of them played together, Paderewski whispered, "Keep going, son. Keep on playing. Don't quit."

So it is with teamwork. Our part may feel just as insignificant as "Chopsticks" being played in a concert hall. But when our tune is enhanced and harmonized by others playing with us, it becomes a beautiful melody.

Making It Personal

What abilities do I have to offer the teams I am part of?

ABCs of Proverbs

*The purpose of these proverbs is to teach people wisdom
and discipline, and to help them understand wise sayings.*
Proverbs 1:2

There is not a book in the Bible that is more down to earth than the book of Proverbs. Proverbs instructs both young and old. It deals with common sense and good manners. It tells what the wise would do in everyday situations. Proverbs is full of tremendous statements that tell us how to live successfully.

To get an overview of the riches found in the book of Proverbs, I want to share the following list of proverbs taken from a little booklet called *The ABC's of Proverbs* published by the American Bible Society. All these verses are taken from the *Good News Bible in Today's English Version.* Reflect carefully on these truths as you read various proverbs over the next few days.

Avoid evil and walk straight ahead. Don't go one step off the right way. (Proverbs 4:27)

Be generous and you will be prosperous. Help others and they will help you. (Proverbs 11:25)

Correction and discipline are good for children. If they have their own way, they will make their mothers ashamed of them. (Proverbs 29:15)

Making It Personal

How can I be more generous?

ABCs of Proverbs

*The purpose of these proverbs is to teach people wisdom
and discipline, and to help them understand wise sayings.*
Proverbs 1:2

Most of the book of Proverbs was written by King Solomon, who at the zenith of his fame was the embodiment of wisdom.

Don't make friends with people who have hot violent tempers. You might learn their habits and not be able to change. (Proverbs 22:24-25)

Enthusiasm without knowledge is not good; impatience will get you into trouble. (Proverbs 19:2)

Friends always show their love. What are brothers for if not to share trouble? (Proverbs 17:17)

God keeps every promise He makes. He is like a shield for all who seek His protection. (Proverbs 30:5)

Hot tempers cause arguments, but patience brings peace. (Proverbs 15:18)

If you refuse to learn you are hurting yourself. If you accept correction you will become wiser. (Proverbs 15:32)

Making It Personal

How is my temper these days?

ABCs of Proverbs

The purpose of these proverbs is to teach people wisdom and discipline, and to help them understand wise sayings.
Proverbs 1:2

The word translated "proverb" comes from a root that seems to mean "to represent" or "be like." So a proverb originally was a comparison or a simile, with some sort of analogy drawn between the natural and spiritual world. Later, it was extended to include any short, pithy saying.

What a **J**oy it is to find just the right word for the right occasion! (Proverbs 15:23)

Kind words bring life, but cruel words crush your spirit. (Proverbs 15:4)

Let other people praise you—even strangers; never do it yourself. (Proverbs 27:2)

Men may make their plans, but God has the last word. (Proverbs 16:1)

Never say something that isn't true. Have nothing to do with lies and misleading words. (Proverbs 4:24)

Old men are proud of their grandchildren, just as children are proud of their parents. (Proverbs 17:6)

Making It Personal

Am I committed to telling the truth?

ABCs of Proverbs

The purpose of these proverbs is to teach people wisdom and discipline, and to help them understand wise sayings.
Proverbs 1:2

The book of Proverbs is written in poetic form. It uses simile and metaphor, the "if, then" format, and parallelism, where the same thought is stated in two ways. Look for these figures of speech as you read through these proverbs.

Pay attention to your teacher and learn all you can. (Proverbs 23:12)

[A **Q**uote from King Solomon.] Being wise is better than being strong; yes, knowledge is more important than strength. (Proverbs 24:5)

If you **R**efuse good advice, you are asking for trouble; follow it and you are safe. (Proverbs 13:13)

Sometimes it takes a painful experience to make us change our ways. (Proverbs 20:30)

Too much honey is bad for you, and so is trying to win too much praise. (Proverbs 25:27)

Making It Personal

Am I teachable and willing to take advice? Why or why not?

ABCs of Proverbs

The purpose of these proverbs is to teach people wisdom and discipline, and to help them understand wise sayings.
Proverbs 1:2

The best way to appreciate the Proverbs is to consider them as general principles, not commands. They need to be considered separately, reading only a few a time.

Unreliable messengers cause trouble, but those who can be trusted bring peace. (Proverbs 13:17)

When someone wrongs you, it is a great **V**irtue to ignore it. (Proverbs 19:11)

When you please the Lord, you can make your enemies into friends. (Proverbs 16:7)

With an **X**, mark the proverbs you need to work on.

You do yourself a favor when you are kind. If you are cruel, you only hurt yourself. (Proverbs 11:17)

Zero in on the advice of King Solomon!

※

Making It Personal

Which proverbs do I need to listen to the most?

Newness Blooming

Forget the former things; do not dwell on the past.
See, I am doing a new thing!
Isaiah 43:18-19 (NIV)

In Dallas, when the jonquils finish blooming and the bluebonnets begin to appear, we know springtime is near. I love this season of year and the new hope and freshness it promises.

Maybe for you the present seems dreary and you are not excited about the future. Isaiah 43:19 is for you, as God says, "See, I am doing a new thing!" Wouldn't you love to do a new thing? Forget the disappointments in your work—the postponed meetings, the missed goals, whatever. It doesn't matter. God is going to do a new thing. What a great promise this is!

Later on in the same chapter of Isaiah, the Lord reminds the Israelites that they had refused to ask for His help. Stubborn people, you say. But are we any different? Those of us who believe in God and yet try to function on our own displease the Lord. The result is not functioning at all.

Let's take heart in this new season of beautiful flowering colors. Let's ask God for wisdom to use the gifts He has given us. And let's believe God will do His new thing!

Making It Personal

What new thing might God want to do for me today?

Spring Forward

[God] gives us rain each spring and fall, assuring us of plentiful harvests.
Jeremiah 5:24

Spring, summer, fall, winter. Most parts of the country experience these seasonal changes in weather every year. We experience seasons in our lives, too.

In the Old Testament book of Ruth we read about Naomi and her two daughters-in-law, Ruth and Orpah. All three women lost their husbands. Naomi wanted to move back to her homeland, and she told her daughters to remain there, in their own land. The young women suddenly faced a tough decision. Orpah decided to stay home, to stay in her comfort zone. Ruth boldly decided to follow Naomi to a new land.

Ruth ventured into a new season of life, full of risk, yes, but also full of new possibilities. Just as the spring rains bring tiny pink buds, little white flowers, and green blades of grass, so these women found new hope after a hard, barren season in their lives.

Maybe you have gone through a personal challenge in your life recently—illness, financial setbacks, hard decisions. I encourage you to take a step into a new spring. Spring always brings change. The choices you make in your "spring time" will impact your life for years to come.

Making It Personal

What risky springtime choices am I facing today?

Neighborhood Service

*Never seek revenge or bear a grudge against
anyone, but love your neighbor as yourself.*
Leviticus 19:18

There was a time when neighbors "neighbored" more than they do today. It wasn't so long ago, in fact. When I was a young wife and mom, my neighbors and I would often visit in the backyard. I also remember going next door to borrow some flour or a cup of sugar. The food was incidental—the visiting together was the important thing.

Our need for socializing is as great as it ever was, perhaps greater. Why do you think coffee shops are so full of people? It's not only to drink all that caffeine or read the newspaper; coffee shops are places to be like a neighbor and be with a neighbor. Sure, you can't borrow groceries there, but you can borrow recipes and swap business ideas.

All of us are eager for a place of community, where we can strengthen relationships and serve each other by offering what we have to give. How can we be better neighbors to each other? How can we see our colleagues as neighbors to be served?

Making It Personal

How can I love my "neighbors" today?

Remember

Give thanks to the LORD and proclaim his greatness. Let the whole world know what he has done. . . . [Remember] the wonderful works he has done.
Psalm 105:1, 5

Remember what God has done!" That is what the Bible tells God's people to do. Remember how:

- ☞ God created the heavens and the earth.
- ☞ God delivered His people out of bondage in Egypt.
- ☞ God provided for all their needs.

When the Israelites were about to enter the Promised Land, Moses urged them never to forget how they had gotten to this new land and who had provided it for them. They were to always remember that the land was a gift from God. As a tangible reminder they set up a pile of memorial stones with the Law written on them. "When you cross the Jordan River and enter the land the Lord your God is giving you, set up some large stones and coat them with plaster. Then write all the terms of this law on them" (Deuteronomy 27:2-3).

God has been so good to us. I want to remind you to remember that. Remember God's amazing works, His tender mercies, and His everlasting, unconditional love.

Making It Personal

Set up your own memorial of "stones," and jot down two things that God has done for you that you want to remember.

Caught!

*Make the most of every opportunity
for doing good in these evil days.*
Ephesians 5:16

I read about a company that made up certificates for its employees. On the front it said, "You've been caught . . ." Turning the page, it read, " . . . doing something good!"

Isn't that great? You could personalize that idea by having cards made up saying, "You've been caught . . . doing something special" or "something creative in your business" or "something really thoughtful." Then write a personal thank-you note for what they've done for you, or acknowledging an accomplishment.

That is building your business from the head to the heart. It's this kind of personal touch that I believe builds unity and strengthens relationships. Make every effort to catch people doing something good.

Making It Personal

Who can I "catch" today doing something special?

Guard Your Reputation

*Choose a good reputation over great riches, for being held
in high esteem is better than having silver or gold.*
Proverbs 22:1

Proverbs 22:1 talks about the importance of building a reputation; and not just any reputation, but a *good* reputation. Just what is a reputation? *Webster's Dictionary* says it is "an overall quality or character as judged by people in general; a recognition by other people of some characteristic or ability." A good reputation is recognized by good actions.

This proverb is really telling us to get our priorities in order. As we live, so we are known. If we live with integrity, then we build a trustworthy reputation. If we live with dishonesty, then eventually our reputation will be a bad one. Once we have lied or cheated, we can no longer be trusted. Once lost, a good reputation is very difficult to regain. Once we lose that trust and respect, it's very hard to undo the damage. Having a good reputation is priceless. Building a good reputation is important—it is who we are!

Making It Personal
What kind of reputation am I building?

He Knows My Days

*You saw me before I was born. Every day of my life was recorded in
your book. Every moment was laid out before a single day had passed.*
Psalm 139:16

The story of Helen Keller has captured the hearts of Americans for a century. Illness robbed her of both sight and hearing when she was nineteen months old. The doctors said she would never see or hear again. Helen Keller's parents were advised by Alexander Graham Bell to contact the Perkins Institute for the Blind in Boston. They contacted Perkins and asked for a teacher for young Helen. On March 3, 1887, Anne Sullivan arrived. The rest of the story is well known. Helen went on to college and graduated from Radcliff, completing the required courses in four years. She learned French, Latin, and German, conquering them with a double disability.

I believe Psalm 139:16, and that God planned every day of my life before I was born. Did God plan every day of the life of that little girl? I believe He did. Did God want her to remain locked in her dark and silent prison for all her days? No, I don't believe so. He had a good plan for her life, even though she was handicapped. God knew her days, and God knows your days too. You can trust His timetable. Don't give up!

Making It Personal

What does it mean to me that God knows my days?

Power of a Fragrance

Our lives are a fragrance presented by Christ to God. But this fragrance is perceived differently by those being saved and by those perishing.
2 Corinthians 2:15

I traveled often with Mary Crowley on various business trips. Before we reached our destination I was in the habit of putting on perfume. She would always say something about it because she did not like perfumes and their heavy smells!

To my surprise, then, one day she gave me a small bottle of perfume. "The next time you are on my plane with me, I want you to use this," she said.

I asked, "Why? You don't like me to use perfume."

"Because it smells like vanilla wafers, and I like those!"

There are some fragrances that are just annoying and can even be deadly—just take a whiff of your trash next time you take it out. And there are some fragrances that are heavenly. Vanilla wafers, fresh bread, the smell of lilacs. Hmmm . . . these are life-giving fragrances!

The Bible tells us that our lives can be like that—a lovely fragrance of Christ's love to others. Be a life-giving fragrance to others today.

Making It Personal

What kind of life-giving fragrance is my life spreading to others?

No Dark Panes

O LORD, you are my light; yes, LORD, you light up my darkness.
2 Samuel 22:29

During a severe storm on a Scottish peninsula, a lighthouse window was broken. The lighthouse keeper, being lazy, boarded up the hole in the window, which also blocked the light on that side. He decided to wait until the next day to fix the window.

That night a ship was blown off course and came upon the rocky peninsula from the dark side of the lighthouse. With no light to warn of danger, the ship crashed upon the rocks. The lighthouse keeper was devastated. He didn't think that the one dark part mattered. *But it always matters.*

Our company's purpose is to light up the homes of America and really make an impact. To do that, the windows of our lives must be clear and shining. We must have no dark panes. You see, any small areas of darkness in our lives do matter. There will be consequences if we don't deal with them.

Do you think your window doesn't matter? Do you think you don't really affect other people? Let me assure you that you do. Learn a lesson from the lighthouse keeper. Keep the windows of your life open and full of light.

Making It Personal

What dark areas in my life do I need to clean up?

Note This

Now here is my greeting, which I write with my own hand—Paul.
2 Thessalonians 3:17

A handwritten note is becoming rather novel. We live in an age of technology and lightning-speed information, surrounded by wireless computers, modems, Palm Pilots,® and, of course, e-mail. Anyone with a computer can pound out e-mail (even me!) or construct letters on a computerized bulletin board (not me!). But the handwritten note says something different to the recipient. When I receive one, it tells me that I am valued and special, and I am uplifted and encouraged. Often I have received a timely note, coming just when I needed it, and I am so grateful.

The former football coach of Notre Dame University, Lou Holtz, was a great note writer. As busy as he was, he always found time to write and thank those who served him, to offer congratulations, or to acknowledge someone in a special way. He encouraged his coaching staff and all his team members to write at least one note a day.

The few minutes it takes to write a friendly note is a wise investment in your relationships, not to mention your business. Try it. You might like it. That's keeping the personal touch.

Making It Personal

Whom can I encourage today with a note?

Wholehearted Commitment

*And you must commit yourselves wholeheartedly to these commands I am
giving you today. Repeat them again and again to your children.*
Deuteronomy 6:6-7

Moses, the leader of the Israelites in ancient times, always stressed the importance of loving God and passing on His laws to succeeding generations. Why did Moses urge the people to keep repeating God's commands over and over to their children? I think he realized how necessary it was to teach the future generations if they were to become the nation God desired. Hear, commit, and then pass it on!

The story is told of a high-school teacher who with great pride often spoke of her teaching career that spanned thirty-eight years. Her principal, however, corrected the record. "Well, she's a first-year teacher thirty-eight times over." Do you see the difference? Each year that teacher was making the same mistakes she made during her first year—mistakes that should have been corrected long ago. She never profited from her past errors. She never had a wholehearted commitment to her teaching profession or to her students.

The moral here? You can't pass on what you are not committed to yourself.

Making It Personal

Am I committed to the right things? What are they?

Take Time to Care

And the King will tell them, "I assure you, when you did it to one of the least of these my brothers and sisters, you were doing it to me!"
Matthew 25:40

Mother Teresa was revered as a living saint, and spent her entire life caring for the poor and less fortunate. She won the Nobel Peace Prize in 1979 and was known around the world for her Christian compassion and love.

The story is told of one occasion when a man with terminal cancer was brought to her. One of the workers vomited because of the man's stench and had to leave. Mother Teresa kindly took over. "How can you stand the smell?" the patient asked. She replied very simply, "It is nothing compared to the pain you must feel." What a personal touch! What a divine love!

While not everyone is called to a full-time ministry to the sick and the poor, every Christian is responsible to care for others. You can call it love, concern, compassion, or care. It all means to have a willingness to reach out, to provide encouragement for others, to just be there.

No matter what business we are in, we have the perfect vehicle to share a personal touch. There are people everywhere who are hurting, lonely, in need of a smile, a dose of hope. Take time to care and to make a difference.

Making It Personal

What things (fears, impatience, lack of time) keep me from really caring for other people?

April

A good reputation is the
result of the choices we make,
so choose a good reputation
over great riches.

With love,
Joan

Play Ball!

*So accept each other just as Christ has
accept you; then God will be glorified.*
Romans 15:7

For those of you who share my love of baseball, today is the MID of the year (Most Important Day). The season begins!

All the spring training is now put to the test. The players must now be relational because they are part of a team. You have heard that there is no "I" in "TEAM." Even the manager must communicate with his team and build personal relationships.

I read recently in an *Executive Leadership* paper the rules that Joe Torre, the New York Yankees manager, has developed over the years:

1. Remember every player has *needs*. Determine what that need is and meet it.
2. Be quick to *praise* after a good play. Simple words of appreciation are powerful.
3. Build a *relationship* with those of different backgrounds.
4. Let your team know you *accept* their different fears, and work to help them grow through them.

What a great way to "keep it personal" as you build your team.

Making It Personal

How can I accept others more and become a team player?

Hope Springs Eternal

*What is faith? It is the confident assurance that
what we hope for is going to happen.*
Hebrews 11:1

Spring is the time for baseball. I love the crack of the bat, the thud of a fastball hitting a catcher's mitt, peanuts, popcorn, and my favorite baseball team, the Texas Rangers.

No other sport evokes such hope every spring as baseball does. Hope for a winning season, hope for a perfect game, hope for a World Series ring. Hope drives those young men from spring training into the regular season, and hope strengthens their desire for next season.

The same can be true for your life and your business. There is always hope for providing for your family, hope for finding a reason to smile again, hope for finding a new way to reach out to others. Hebrews 11:1 says that hope is closely aligned with faith. You can have confidence that what you hope for is going to happen.

Making It Personal

What do I hope for? Am I confident it will happen?

Listening from Your Head to Your Heart

Listen closely to what I am saying. You can console me by listening to me.
Job 21:2

You've heard the phrase, "*From your head to your heart.*" This simple phrase is actually a rather complex statement about two opposites. The *head* deals with facts, knowledge, no variances, adherence to rules and regulations, logic. The *heart* deals with feelings, compassion, some variances, serving, encouraging, emotions.

Let's put this phrase in the context of your business. How do you build a business *from* your head *to* your heart? I suggest we need to go through some doorways. Now a doorway is a small thing we often take for granted, but without a doorway you can't get anywhere!

To move from the head to the heart, the first doorway we need to walk through is *listening*. We must make it a priority to listen carefully—to our families, friends, hostesses. Listening allows us to know in our heads what people's needs are, and then our hearts can reach out to fill the need.

Give people your full attention and listen to what is said and what is *not* said. If we want to build from the head to the heart, we must go through the doorway of listening.

Making It Personal

How can I build my business, and my life, from my head to my heart?

Speaking from Your Head to Your Heart

May the words of my mouth and the thoughts of my heart
be pleasing to you, O LORD, my rock and my redeemer.
Psalm 19:14

The second doorway we need to walk through to move our business from our heads to our hearts is the door of our mouths—speaking. How often we regret words we have spoken rashly! The Bible tells us that whatever is in our heart determines what we say.

Before you speak, ask yourself: Are my words accurate or are they exaggerated? Are they necessary? Are they helpful? Are they true? Am I a part of the solution or am I adding to the problem? Am I being grateful or complaining?

Maybe we don't need to talk so much. Our chances of blowing it are directly proportional to the amount of time we spend with our mouths open. Try closing it for awhile. When you do speak, speak from your head through your heart.

Making It Personal

Do I blurt with my mouth, or do I speak through my heart?

Serving from Your Head to Your Heart

Never be lazy in your work, but serve the Lord enthusiastically.
Romans 12:11 (*Verse of the Year 1991*)

Going from our heads to our hearts, we need to walk through a third doorway—serving. This is the very foundation of a "head-to-heart" business.

So many people sacrifice service for speed. We're in too much of a hurry to be polite. There are so many rude people out there. Our telephone calls are put on "hold"—they are really put on "ignore!" There's a lack of interest in serving. That lack might come from a head-oriented, just-the-facts business, but it does not come from a heart business.

Service is not tangible like jewelry. Service doesn't take up shelf space; it can't be invented, appreciated, and taxed. Service doesn't exist until it is needed. But service can be modeled just as our jewelry can. It can be demonstrated. When the customer is satisfied and really pleased to be doing business with us, then we have built from the head to the heart.

Making It Personal

In what way can I be more service-oriented?

Personal Touch from Your Head to Your Heart

Be sure to do what you should, for then you will enjoy the personal satisfaction of having done your work well.
Galatians 6:4

We've talked about some ways to move your business from your head to your heart through listening, speaking, and serving. I want to reflect on a fourth area that means so much to me: *a warm personal touch*. We experience a whole new world when we walk through this doorway, truly building our business from the head to the heart!

We all have the responsibility to listen—in a personal way; to speak—in a personal way; and to serve—with a personal touch. Take that personal time. Remember that your business is people, and we have a wonderful opportunity to offer emotional support and that personal touch from the head to the heart.

In order for Premier Designs to be different, this "heart" touch must begin with you. If you have a relationship problem with another coworker, building from the head to the heart means that you can meet that person for lunch. Talk over the difficulties, and if comfortable, pray together. Invest love, encouragement, and the personal touch, and it will help you build a successful business, and a successful life.

Making It Personal

What situation am I facing right now that needs a personal touch?

The Gold Standard

*Do for others what you would like them to do for you. This is a
summary of all that is taught in the law and the prophets.*
Matthew 7:12

Gold has been used for thousands of years to make precious jewelry. It can be melted down and used over and over again. Gold does not rust or tarnish and cannot corrode. One ounce of gold can be drawn into a wire more than fifty miles long.

Merchants began giving their gold to the goldsmiths for safekeeping and they received paper receipts for their gold. These receipts were easier to carry, much safer, and just as negotiable as the gold itself. The goldsmiths became our very first bankers. Because of its durability and beauty and value, gold is used worldwide as the standard for monetary purposes.

Because gold is so precious, it has come to be synonymous with richness, warmth, and beauty. We speak of golden sunsets, golden harvests, the golden years, a heart of gold, good as gold. And there's no better gold standard to live by than the Golden Rule: "Do unto others as you would have them do unto you."

Making It Personal

When have I experienced the value of living by the Golden Rule?

Love Is a Verb

*Dear children, let us stop just saying we love each other;
let us really show it by our actions.*
1 John 3:18 (Verse of the Year 2004)

How easy it is for us to casually say "I love you" to family and friends, but what does that mean? What am I saying when I tell you that I love you? This verse in the book of 1 John helps us out. In plain language it tells us, "Don't just talk about love; *practice* love." Don't stop at just saying the words—that's merely lip service. We are to show our love by our actions, our gifts, and our service.

Love can be both a noun and a verb. The feelings and idea of love (the noun) can only be known from the actions (love, the verb) that result from it. In the verse above, love is used as a verb—a word of action. Loving each other means we are doing something, not just speaking words.

So how do we "do" love? With our hands of service, with our money and material goods, with our time and talents, with our speech, and with our countenance. Get out there and love!

Making It Personal
What is one way I can "do" love today?

Guests of Honor

Martha welcomed them into her home. Her sister, Mary, sat at the Lord's feet, listening to what he taught. But Martha was worrying over the big dinner she was preparing.
Luke 10:38-40

When Martha welcomed Jesus and the disciples to her home, it could have been all twelve of His disciples, or maybe only two. We don't know. I have been to Israel and seen the archaeological sites of homes in Christ's time. A typical house then was quite small. So where did all Martha's visitors go? Yet, she welcomed them. Then she worried about the big dinner she was preparing. Well, I would worry, too! And I believe Martha could expect a little help. After all, it was Mary's home, too.

Jesus was quick to put things in perspective for Martha. All the necessary busyness that was preoccupying her really didn't matter in the end. *Jesus was there*. He was to be the focus. Martha was passing up a tremendous opportunity to learn from Him.

Anyone who knows me knows that I love to host dinner parties. This story reminds me that entertaining guests is not about that good dinner or awesome chocolate chip cake I may serve. It's not even about my home or how I look. Rather, it is about honoring my guests and meeting their needs. It all goes back to my passion for keeping it personal!

Making It Personal

Do I worry more about my image than about people? Why?

Integrity in Leadership

*I know, my God, that you examine our hearts
and rejoice when you find integrity there.*
1 Chronicles 29:17

What makes a good leader? Consider Thomas Jefferson, Henry Ford, or Martin Luther King. Jefferson wrote the Declaration of Independence. Ford gave us a vehicle that made us independent. King gave us a dream for freedom.

Each one was a dreamer and yet practical; an original, yet totally in sync with his peers. Each of these leaders did something new. They all had the ingredients for good leadership: integrity, dedication, humility, openness, creativity, and the ability to dream great dreams.

One basic ingredient of leadership is *integrity*. Integrity is more than just being honest; it's a standard of moral honesty that governs our conduct. It means to be the same through and through, inside and outside. This is the quality that is diluted and almost absent from many corporations and government offices today. In order to restore our nation's integrity, each individual must have personal integrity—it's that simple.

To have integrity in our company as a whole, each person must operate with a sense of integrity and live as a vital example of that standard.

Making It Personal

Am I known as a person of integrity?

Teamwork

Two people can accomplish more than twice as much as one;
they get a better return for their labor.
Ecclesiastes 4:9

Baseball great Nolan Ryan said of his wife, "Ruth has always been there for me, always backing me up, always covering home." As members of a business team, are we backing each other up? Are we always covering home? It takes teamwork.

T is for togetherness. Work with others rather than individually.

E is for empathy. Be interested in your team members.

A is for assisting. Help others when they need it.

M is for maturity. Handle problems in a positive manner—don't blame others.

W is for willingness. Be ready to work with others.

O is for organization. Being organized makes you a less stressed-out team player.

R is for respect. Have respect for the people on your team.

K is for kindness. Be kind to people with whom you work.

That is the kind of team that will work!

Making It Personal

How can I be a team player and "cover home" for others?

April 12

Uplifting Notes

*Your friends here send you their greetings. Please give my
personal greetings to each of our friends there.*
3 John 1:15

I prefer to write my letters by hand. I must admit it is getting increasingly more difficult. But when people are promoted up the ladder of leadership, I want them to know we notice their achievements. They are encouraged when they receive a little note of appreciation, and I will continue to do this as long as I have breath. That is part of my commitment to "keeping it personal."

Why do I say "handwritten" note? Because that's the personal touch we all long for. We all need that personal touch. The notes don't have to be long— in fact the shorter the better. I believe it is a wise investment for your business. It builds unity and strengthens relationships.

In a society that is becoming more and more impersonal, our work places need to be places where people feel appreciated and needed. People really want to feel affirmation, support, and love. They want that personal touch. What a difference it makes when we can respond in such a way that we can comfort and encourage, uplift and support, affirm and love. We want to make a difference in their lives—with our personal touch.

Making It Personal

Am I too busy to write personal notes to encourage someone today?

Service That Meets a Need

*People curse those who hold their grain for higher prices,
but they bless the one who sells to them in their time of need.*
Proverbs 11:26

Colonial America was mostly rural. People lived in settlements far apart, with no shopping malls close by. They got their sundry supplies from "Yankee peddlers," called that because they came from Connecticut. In effect, the Yankee peddlers were the founders of "direct sales." These folks would fill up their wagons with supplies the country people needed, and travel from town to town, house to house. The Yankee peddlers provided a service and met a real need.

During the 1930s and 1940s, many companies sprang up using the door-to-door method of direct selling. The ones who maintained their success were those who not only sold a product but also met a need and provided good service. Those principles of long ago can still be applied today. In our business, here's what we can take away from the Yankee peddlers:

1. "You can't work from an empty wagon." You have to have *quality merchandise.*
2. You have to have merchandise that people *want and need.*
3. You have to take it *where people are.*

Making It Personal

What can I learn from the Yankee peddlers?

Riches or Reputation?

*Choose a good reputation over great riches, for being held
in high esteem is better than having silver or gold.*
Proverbs 22:1

P art of having a good reputation comes from living well.
With that in mind, we must be careful of the many
hindrances to building an honorable reputation. One of
them can be the lure of riches. Seldom do you read of a
person who "has it all" and also has the most important
ingredient in success—a good reputation.

The Bible gives us many examples of prosperous
people who did not lose their integrity. The classic example
is David. He went from shepherd to king before he was
thirty years old. Enormous power and riches. How did he
handle it? "God took David from tending the ewes and
lambs and made him the shepherd of Jacob's descendants.
. . . He cared for them with a true heart and led them with
skillful hands" (Psalm 78:71-72). The New King James
Version says that he led them "according to the integrity
of his heart." Awesome!

How do we handle prosperity? Is making lots of money
more important than being trustworthy and having integrity?
A good reputation is the result of the choices we make, so
choose a good reputation over great riches.

Making It Personal

What is more important to me—riches or reputation? Why?

Easter Renewal

Do not be so surprised. You are looking for Jesus, the Nazarene, who was crucified. He isn't here! He has been raised from the dead!
Mark 16:6

Spring is always such a special time of renewal for me. The bluebonnets and Bradford pear blossoms arrive and everything seems to be in bloom.

One of my favorite parts of spring is Easter. What could be a more beautiful sign of new beginnings than Easter? The common symbol of Easter that we see in stores—the Easter egg—is a symbol of new life. Did you know that Easter eggs have been around since the nineteenth century? Czar Alexander III commissioned master goldsmith Peter Carl Faberge to make beautiful eggs to use as gifts in celebration of special dates. The first egg was designed in 1885 and was given as an Easter gift. So the eggs that we give at Easter remind us of the renewal God offers us.

More important, though, is that Easter is the time Christians celebrate Jesus' resurrection from the dead! Jesus was crucified, but on the third day, he rose again. Hallelujah! What a tremendous reminder of God's mighty power to break even the bonds of death. Through Christ, He gives us all a fresh new beginning.

Making It Personal

What does Easter mean to me?

April 16

Believe in What You Do

The LORD has given them special skills as jewelers, designers, weavers, and embroiderers. . . . They excel in all the crafts needed for the work.
Exodus 35:35

My husband, Andy, and I love what we do. We enjoy working with and serving people, and we believe deeply in the Philosophy and Purpose of our business.

We founded our business on biblical principles, and we continue to operate on those same principles. Our confidence lies not in the sales figures, the new buildings, or our fabulous leadership, though these are all tremendous blessings. But our real confidence comes from believing that what we are doing has purpose and meaning. Because of our dependence on the Lord and His Word, we work hard at our jobs.

Mary Crowley used to say, "Find something to do that you love so much, you will do it for free. Then learn to be so good at it that the world will pay you well to do it." If you work for the thing you believe in, you're already rich, though the way may be rough. If you're working only for money, you can never earn quite enough!

So work hard for the satisfaction of a job well done, and for the opportunity to serve and enrich others.

Making It Personal

What motivates me in my work?

Good Plans

*"For I know the plans I have for you," says the LORD. "They are plans
for good and not for disaster, to give you a future and a hope."*
Jeremiah 29:11

It's easy to lose hope when our circumstances turn out
quite different from what we planned. The people of
Israel knew this hopeless feeling all too well.

Due to their disobedience, they were conquered and
taken into exile by the Babylonians. While they were in
exile, the prophet Jeremiah spoke the word of the Lord:
" 'You will be in Babylon for seventy years. But then I will
come and do for you all the good things I have promised.
. . . For I know the plans I have for you,' says the LORD"
(Jeremiah 29:10-11).

After seventy years. They were stuck in those
circumstances for a long time, but THEN . . . God would
come and do what He said! How did this give them hope?
Because God reminded them that He was in control, "I
know the plans I have for you . . . "

Maybe you don't know what is happening in your
life. But our omniscient God knows all. Maybe you are
discouraged and feeling hopeless. But our good God is the
source of hope. When you need hope, Jeremiah's words
are a good place to start: "I know the plans I have for you,"
God says. You can trust that His plans are always good!

Making It Personal

How does knowing that God is in control give me hope today?

Truths Worth Knowing

Hallelujah! For the Lord our God, the Almighty, reigns.
Revelation 19:6

One of my heroes is Joni Earekson Tada. A quadra-plegic, Joni heads up a worldwide ministry that includes painting, speaking, writing, advocating for the handicapped, and providing wheelchairs to people who need them. We have had the privilege of visiting with her several times, and I am always uplifted and encouraged when I am with her. Joni has a very real and down-to-earth faith.

After living in a wheelchair for years, she could be bitter and angry. But the following truths from God's Word are burned into her heart and soul, and she loves to share them:

1. God is in control.
2. He leads me along a path He has planned.
3. Nothing can touch me that is not in His plan.
4. He is passionate about my highest good.
5. His grace is available and abundant.

We are all disabled in one way or another. We all need to know God's love and grace in our lives. Let these truths sink deep into your heart today.

Making It Personal

Which of these truths about God do I wrestle with the most? Why?

Faith in the Marketplace

*Jesus told him, "If you want to be perfect, go and sell
all you have and give the money to the poor, and you will have
treasure in heaven. Then come, follow me."*
Matthew 19:21

Peter Waldo was a prosperous merchant who lived in Lyons, France, in the twelfth century. A devout Christian, he felt called to renounce his property and distribute the remainder of his wealth to the poor. Petrus Valdesius, as his Latin name was called, then began preaching the gospel in the streets of Lyons. To finance his mission, he later eventually returned to his prior business as a merchant, while he continued preaching.

His followers later became known as the Waldensians. As a Waldensian preacher and merchant traveled to the local manors, the townspeople gathered around while he showed his jewelry and other wares. He then talked to them about even more precious goods in his possession— spiritual jewels of inestimable value!

These peddlers used the selling of jewelry to support themselves, and the jewelry also provided them an avenue of ministry to people they met. Hence, their business became a means to honor God. They were living out their faith in the marketplace.

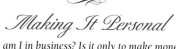

Making It Personal

*Why am I in business? Is it only to make money,
or to serve others as well?*

Pearl of Great Price

*Jesus said, "The Kingdom of Heaven is like a pearl merchant on
the lookout for choice pearls. When he discovered a pearl of great value,
he sold everything he owned and bought it!"*
Matthew 13:45-46

John Greenleaf Whittier, the nineteenth-century Quaker
poet, wrote a poem based on accounts of the medieval
Waldensians, the traveling merchants and preachers. As
the audience showed curiosity about their jewelry and
wares, the Waldensian would then speak of the "pearl of
great price," the kingdom of God.

> *O lady fair, I have yet a gem,*
> *Which a purer luster flings*
> *Than the diamond flash of the jeweled crown,*
> *On the lofty brow of kings.*
>
> *A wonderful pearl of exceeding price,*
> *Whose virtue shall not decay,*
> *Whose light shall be as a spell to thee,*
> *And a blessing on thy way.*

Do you see what they were doing? First of all, they
offered gems for sale. (These must have been some of the
earliest Home Shows ever recorded!) Then they offered
the richest gem of all: the precious gospel of Christ.

Making It Personal

What do I value above all else?

Made to Count

For it pleased God in his kindness to choose me and call me,
even before I was born! What undeserved mercy!
Galatians 1:15

One of the most powerful books I have read is *Made to Count* by Bob Reccord and Randy Singer. Page after page is filled with inspiring stories of folks who have followed God's plan to serve others in one way or another.

There are marvelous accounts of business people who, even through mistakes and difficulties, have made significant contributions to society. There are other stories of how ordinary people, who finally yielded their lives to God's love and power, were changed forever. God's calling was always there, for they were "made to count."

We have all been created to make a difference. We are all made to count for something unique. Our story may not ever be noticed or published in a book, but God sees and knows, and that's all that matters. Ask God what He is calling you to do in your sphere of influence.

Making It Personal

How can I make a unique difference in someone's life?

Pass It On

*Teach these great truths to trustworthy people
who are able to pass them on to others.*
2 Timothy 2:2

Horses are domesticated animals with many great qualities. They are beautiful, smart, and fast. Horses reproduce other fast horses. Donkeys are not nearly so beautiful nor as fast, but they are very strong and have great stamina. Donkeys beget other strong donkeys. A mule is a sterile offspring of a female horse and a male donkey. It can carry heavy loads, but mules are sterile and cannot reproduce.

This analogy breaks down quickly when we are talking about people, of course! But you probably know some people in your business who are really smart and fast. They are like shooting stars taking off and will bring in others who will do the same. You may have a few on your team who are plodders, slower but with great stamina. And you may have some competent but "sterile" folks on your team, who won't reproduce much at all.

If you want to lead, it's up to you to carry on the vision. You must build a strong team of "horses" who are ready to reproduce, build on what they've learned, and take it to the next level.

Making It Personal

What vision do I need to pass on to others in my business?

Friends for Different Seasons

*There is a time for everything, a season for every activity
under heaven. . . . A time to cry and a time to laugh.*
Ecclesiastes 3:1, 4

We need friends at all stages of our lives. We need other women to come alongside and speak our language. We learn from each other and challenge each other. And sometimes we need different friends for different seasons of life.

During our years working at Home Interiors and Gifts, we worked with thousands of amazing women, many of whom became good friends and encouraged us greatly. When we left that company, Andy was relieved, as he was burned out. But I was devastated and suffered withdrawal pains. Many of my personal friendships across the country were abruptly severed. I was hurting badly and there was nothing I could do about it. I needed a good dose of that personal touch.

God did exceedingly above anything I could ask or think. In time, He turned many of the Premier Designs Jewelers, who were once all strangers, into dear friends! The friendships in Premier have richly blessed me. I believe God used that experience of loss in my life to show me the importance of having a friendly, personal touch in all our lives.

Making It Personal

Who has been a dear friend to me in a hard season of life?

Let's Celebrate!

*This is the LORD's doing and it is marvelous to see. This is the day
the LORD has made. We will rejoice and be glad in it.*
Psalm 118:23-24 (Verse of the Year 2005)

The word *celebrate* has different meanings to different folks. Couples celebrate being married for sixty years with a special cruise or trip. First-time parents celebrate their new baby with a baby shower. Texas Rangers' fans celebrate sweeping the Yankees with a blow-out party! There are countless other reasons for celebrating: A sixteenth birthday and that first driver's license, a Bar Mitzvah or Bat Mitzvah, graduations, and weddings.

Many celebrations are recorded in the Bible. Harvest time was celebrated with offerings and songs and parades of produce. Deborah sang a joyous song to celebrate victory in battle, as did Moses and Miriam. Hannah sang a song of thanks for answered prayer. David danced to celebrate the return of the Ark of the Covenant to God's people. Mary celebrated her news from the angel that she would bear God's Son with one of the loveliest songs recorded, the Magnificat.

On occasions like these, the people paused to enjoy God's good gifts and to give thanks for what He had done in their lives. The Bible encourages us to be joyous people. How are you at celebrating?

Making It Personal

When was the last time I had a good celebration?

Hearing with Understanding

*So the people went away to . . . celebrate with great joy
because they had heard God's words and understood them.*
Nehemiah 8:12

I've read this story in the book of Nehemiah many times, always focusing on "the joy of the LORD is your strength" part in Nehemiah 8:10. What I am guilty of is not really seeing the whole context.

After listening to the Book of the Law of God, which had been ignored for many years, the people wept with remorse. It was then that Nehemiah told them, "Go and celebrate with a feast of choice foods and sweet drinks, . . . For today is a sacred day before the LORD your God. Don't be dejected and sad, for the joy of the LORD is your strength!"

The people went away to eat and share gifts and celebrate. Further on we are told that, "Everyone was filled with great joy! The Israelites had not celebrated this way since the days of Joshua." How could they celebrate even in the midst of remorse? *Because they had heard God's words and understood them.* God's Word always speaks truth in love, and truth leads to true joy.

Making It Personal

Am I really hearing and understanding God's Word for my life?

Build a Bridge

*"I wanted to build a Temple to honor the name
of the LORD my God," David told him.*
1 Chronicles 22:7

Through our business and the hard work of many people, Andy and I have had many wonderful opportunities to build bridges of hope for others, for which we are grateful.

The bridge reaches out to people who need to make a living. The bridge reaches across to upstate New York to a camp for at-risk kids. The bridge goes to Mexico, helping build a needed orphanage. Many countries around the world are seeing that bridge of opportunity, hope, and love. Lord willing, those bridges will continue to be built as God shows us the needs. What a joy to be part of God's bridge-building plan!

No matter where you live or what you do, you can be in the bridge-building business too. When you face disappointments, keep on building, serving, and caring. When you want to quit, keep on building, serving, and caring. Reach out and build bridges of hope and opportunity.

Making It Personal

What kind of bridges am I building in my relationships? In my work?

Know the Times

*From the tribe of Issachar, there were 200 leaders of the tribe
with their relatives. All these men understood the temper of the times
and knew the best course for Israel to take.*
1 Chronicles 12:32

In this Old Testament story we read about the thousands of men who swore allegiance to David as the new king of Israel. These men were valiant warriors. They were well equipped with spears and shields. Some were expert archers and they could shoot arrows or sling stones with their left hand as well as their right. They were all fully armed and ready to fight beside David.

Hidden in the list is a side note about the leaders from the tribe of Issachar, who "understood the temper of the times and knew the best course for Israel to take." Isn't that amazing? All 200 men were tuned in to the situation. They understood the real issues at hand. And they wisely agreed on the best course to take. What leader wouldn't want these kinds of followers?

Part of making wise decisions today is being prepared and ready for anything. But even better is to know the temper of the times in which we live and make good choices.

Making It Personal

*What are some of the major issues of our culture today
that I am concerned about?*

Steps to Success

*Whoever wants to be a leader among you must be your servant
and whoever wants to be first must become your slave.*
Matthew 20:26-27

The longer I live, the more I see that Jesus' words in the verses above are true for life, for work, for relationships. My husband, Andy, once outlined ten basic steps for being successful. Over the next few readings, I want to share these steps with you.

1. Learn to *serve*. If you want to succeed—in God's eyes—then learn what it means to serve. Jesus showed us what it means to be a servant.

2. Find your *security* in something bigger than yourself. Jesus said, "I give them eternal life, and they will never perish. . . . No one can take them from me. " (John 10:28-30). Our security is not in our business; our security is in Christ. We get our esteem from this.

3. Build on a sure *foundation*. "Now anyone who builds on that good foundation may use gold, silver, jewels, wood, hay or straw. But . . . everyone's work will be put through the fire to see whether or not it keeps its value" (1 Corinthians 3:12-13). Build upon the rock of God's Word and your foundation will hold.

Making It Personal

In what do I find my security?

More Steps to Success

Be careful how you act.
Ephesians 5:15 (TLB) (*Verse of the Year 1993*)

Here are more steps to success.

4. Cultivate *discernment*. We are living in tough times and we need to be wise and discerning. Matthew 7:21 says not all people who sound religious are really godly. James 1:5 says, "If you need wisdom—if you want to know what God wants you to do—ask him, and he will gladly tell you."

5. Be careful how you *live*. Ephesians 5 says that we should walk in love, in light, and with joy and thanksgiving.

6. Have *accountability* in your life. Find honest friends who will tell you when you're wrong. This is the way of growth. For we will all be held accountable later for what we say and do. "You must give an account on judgment day of every idle word you speak" (Matthew 12:36).

Making It Personal

How can I become more discerning?

Final Steps to Success

Yes, I am the vine; you are the branches. Those who remain in me, and I in them, will produce much fruit. For apart from me you can do nothing.
John 15:5

Reflect on these final steps to success. These ten basics will make you a better person, a better leader, and a better businesswoman.

7. Think about *what Jesus would do* in your situation. He had compassion on people, comforted them, and met their needs. He led by example and teaching. How can you emulate Him?

8. *Don't seek glory* and reward. Don't do things so you'll be noticed. Matthew 6:3 says, "When you give to someone, don't tell the left hand what your right hand is doing." And Luke 12:48 reminds us, "Much is required from those to whom much is given."

9. Have *unity*. In your work and relationships, strive for togetherness—unity in purpose, not necessarily in personalities.

10. *Abide* in Christ. Realize that you cannot do anything by yourself. You need God's strength and power.

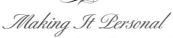

Making It Personal

Which of these steps to success do I need to begin implementing?

May

If you are a mother, take that job seriously and train your children well.

With love,
Joan

After the Rain

For the winter is past, and the rain is over and gone.
Song of Solomon 2:11

The flowers of spring go through a long process to show their beautiful colors. The seeds are buried in the cold ground through winter and pounded by rains and winds in spring. But after the rains, the colors come.

We go through a similar process spiritually. Some of us have strong winds of grief blowing on us right now, making our hearts heavy. Some of us are enduring the devastating rains of a crisis. Some days we feel as if we are drowning.

Difficulties are all a part of life. But the sunshine of God's love and providence can still shine through, bringing the colors of the rainbow. This is the hope God offers in the midst of the rainy season.

Making It Personal

When have I experienced the spiritual "colors of spring"
as a result of a difficult season?

Get Involved

I command you to love each other in the same way that I love you.
John 15:12

When strength fails and illness comes, when we grow weary and discouraged, when the bills pile up and money runs short, we don't need another e-mail, we need a real person to come alongside us, to offer understanding or cheer us up. We all need that personal touch at some time or other.

Who is our example of that personal touch? Of course, it is Lord Jesus Himself. In Mark 1:40-41 a man with leprosy came to Jesus for healing. "If you want to, you can make me well again," the man said. Jesus said, "I want to. Be healed!" In other words, "Yes! I want to get personally involved, I want to touch you and help you." Jesus went where people were and He had a personal touch—in the marketplace, in the boats of the fishermen, in the synagogues, in homes. How can we do less?

I want to be known as a person who cares. That means I have to get personally involved. Will you join me?

Making It Personal

**Who can I call today and give a personal
word of encouragement?**

Weed Your Garden

Children are a gift from the LORD; they are a reward from him.
Psalm 127:3

Every garden has weeds along with the flowers, and thus needs constant weeding and care. Our families are like that. What weeds are we allowing to grow in our children's lives? In our marriages? If you are not married, what weeds are growing in your closest relationships?

We have to dig up the weeds that can choke out family relationships. One of the most difficult weeds in families today is the telephone and the ubiquitous cell phone. This telephone weed is a tough one to pull out. One way you can fight against it is to keep mealtimes sacred. Give your family your undivided attention. Put on the automatic answering machine and make it known that the phone will not be answered at mealtime. Your business can be "closed" during that time.

This is so important. I speak from experience, having raised five children, all of whom were very active teenagers. They knew mealtime was Horner family time. They knew Friday nights were our family night.

Believe me, as your kids get older (and busier) that time shrinks and becomes more precious. So guard it with your life, and watch the weeds die.

Making It Personal

What steps can I take to weed out distractions and guard time with my family?

Friends from Strangers

A friend is always loyal, and a brother is born to help in time of need.
Proverbs 17:17

Many women complain that they don't have many friends. Well then, we need to turn strangers into friends, as the old saying goes! We all start as complete strangers, and by taking a little bit of initiative and taking a personal interest in someone's life, we can start and nurture lasting friendships. There are several ways for us to turn strangers into friends.

First, spend time together, enjoying each other's company, face-to-face.

Second, make personal phone calls. So much is communicated by our voices. My friends will say, "You sound so tired today." Or "Wow, you must have had a wonderful day." Or "Is there something going on? I can tell by your voice." We can hear so much on the phone.

Third, write encouraging notes to your friends, (OK, I'll allow e-mail notes too!) But I still believe that writing from our hearts with pen and paper is more revealing to the reader than electronic communication.

Keeping it personal is vital to building friendships that will last. Not one of us can do it alone. We must all continue that personal touch.

Making It Personal

How can I reach out to a "stranger" today and make a friend?

Not to Be Served

I, the Son of Man, came here not to be served but to serve others.
Mark 10:45

In Jesus' model of service noted in the verse above, I can handle the "to serve others" part okay, but the "not to be served" part really challenges me. I often want others to serve me. And I'm afraid that is the prevailing attitude in the world today.

When do we become cross and upset? It's usually when we expect to be served and are disappointed. Ever sit down in a restaurant and have to wait for all of three minutes for someone to come take your order? We're thinking, *Where are they? Don't they know I'm here to be served?*

When we are upset by little things like this, it shows that our focus is backwards. I am not saying that we should have no feelings, but I am saying that our spirit should be one of service. Then we would not be upset so easily.

As women in business, there is no nobler path to follow than that of service. Our teacher and example is the Lord Himself.

Making It Personal

Today, in what situation can I give up my self-centered desires to help someone else?

J-O-Y

*I have told you this so that you will be filled
with my joy. Yes, your joy will overflow!*
John 15:11

Do you want to know what gives me joy? How about when the Texas Rangers win the pennant? That's real joy for me, right? Well, I would be ecstatic if that happened this season. But if they lost the next season, then I'd lose my joy again. So that's not what gives me joy.

Or maybe it's eating Mexican food in Dallas after being away from home for two weeks. I love Mexican food. That has to be real joy, right? No, it's only a temporary fix.

Or maybe I experience joy when the sales figures our company has posted look great. That does make me happy for all the people in our business, but that's not real joy.

Real joy can be spelled this way:

    J — Jesus first
    O — Others in between
    Y — Yourself last

Seek real, lasting joy through serving the Lord and serving others.

Making It Personal

How would I define real joy?

Curb Your Tongue

I will watch what I do and not sin in what I say. I will curb my tongue.
Psalm 39:1

In an English churchyard a tombstone reads like this:

> *Beneath this stone, a lump of clay,*
> *Lies Arabella Young,*
> *Who on the 24th of May*
> *Began to hold her tongue.*

The tongue is volatile. Washington Irving said, "A sharp tongue is the only tool whose edge grows keener with constant use." James wrote in the Bible, "People can tame all kinds of animals and birds and reptiles and fish, but no one can tame the tongue. It is an uncontrollable evil, full of deadly poison" (James 3:8).

As long as we live, we will never fully control our tongue. We can, however, keep it in check. Here's how to curb your tongue:

1. Think first. Before your lips start moving, ask yourself, *Are my words accurate, exaggerated, kind, sarcastic, necessary, truthful, grateful, or critical?*
2. Talk less. Compulsive talkers find it difficult to keep friends.
3. Start today. Muzzle your tongue now! Poor Arabella Young waited too long.

Making It Personal

What do I need to do to curb my tongue today?

When Things Go Wrong

Even though the fig trees have no blossoms, . . . yet I will rejoice in the LORD!
Habakkuk 3:17-18

The prophet Habakkuk lived during a time when God's people were under attack by their enemy, the cruel Assyrian empire. Things were very bad. Notice all the problems: no buds on the fig trees, no grapes on the vine, a failed olive crop, no produce from the fields, no sheep nor cattle in the barn—and yet the prophet rejoices in his God!

Even though our problems are not the same as Habakkuk's (how many barren fig trees have stressed you out?), they are just as pressing. The important lesson from this passage is the manner in which the prophet reacts to this disaster.

- He determines to make the best of his circumstances. "I will rejoice" and "I will be joyful."
- He affirms his steady faith. "The Sovereign Lord is my strength."
- He trusts in God's provision and enabling. "He will make me as surefooted as a deer."

Try personalizing this passage, replacing the prophet's situation with your own. Then use Habakkuk's ending, knowing that God is sovereign and in control.

Making It Personal

When things go badly in my life, in what do I trust?

Mother's Day

Charm is deceptive, and beauty does not last; but a woman who fears the LORD will be greatly praised.
Proverbs 31:30

The very first Mother's Day in the United States was celebrated in 1905 in West Virginia. In 1914, President Woodrow Wilson issued a proclamation designating the second Sunday in May as "Mother's Day," and it thus became a national holiday. It was a day to be set aside to express our love for all the mothers of our country.

Other countries have revered their mothers also. Napoleon once said, "Let France have good mothers and she will have good sons." In England, Mothering Sunday was a time for family reunions and for the family to be especially attentive to their mothers.

A wonderful passage, Proverbs 31, speaks about the godly woman. Many qualities are mentioned, but the mother's activities begin and conclude with her family. In verse 30, we are told that others praise her. She is best of all! Proverbs 31:30 says it this way, "Charm is deceptive, and beauty does not last; but a woman who fears the LORD will be greatly praised."

Making It Personal

What woman do I know who fears the Lord above all things?

A Mother's Advice

*These are the sayings of King Lemuel,
an oracle that his mother taught him.*
Proverbs 31:1

The final chapter in the book of Proverbs is only twenty-one verses, but it sure packs a wallop! King Lemuel is quoting his mother, so it is from a feminine viewpoint. Ancient Jewish custom was for fathers to teach the sons, but mothers also had great wisdom and influence, as we see in the first eight verses of Proverbs 31.

Her advice revolved around three areas: women, wine, and justice. She warned her son against falling for the wrong woman. I remember when my two sons began dating. I had some advice for them concerning women, because I am one! I had their best interests at heart, as did Lemuel's mother. Then she warned him about the subtle dangers of alcohol that could ruin his effectiveness. Finally, she urged him to fight for justice for the poor and oppressed. Not bad advice from Mom! We can only hope that Lemuel was smart and followed it.

If you are a mother, take that role seriously and use it to teach and train your sons and daughters.

Making It Personal

What one piece of advice would I give my son or daughter today?

What a Woman!

Who can find a virtuous and capable wife?
She is worth more than precious rubies.
Proverbs 31:10

I have always loved Proverbs 31, with teachings from a mother to her son. The amazing "superwoman" described here probably never existed, but she can serve as an example for us moms. This passage spans the depth and breadth of a woman's relationships:

- With her husband—she earns his confidence and praise.
- With her family—she watches over the affairs of the home.
- With those she works with—she works hard and creates a profit.
- With those in need—she opens her arms to people beyond her acquaintance.

"A mother is truth with a map in her hand, beauty with a cake in the oven, wisdom with a confused bank account, and a miracle of love with a sick child in her arms," my dear friend Mary Crowley used to say. I admire and respect working mothers. What a job they have before them! I salute them. And I especially honor single mothers, who are doing the job of both parents.

Making It Personal

How can I become more like the woman of Proverbs 31?

Time Enough

Teach us to make the most of our time, so that we may grow in wisdom.
Psalm 90:12

Every May 12 I pass another milestone—I have a birthday. Time has a way of flying by, doesn't it? I mean, it goes by *F-A-S-T!*

Sometimes we complain of an acquaintance or colleague who engaged us in conversation, "She took so much of my time!" In saying that, we are acknowledging that time is our greatest possession. We are like Napoleon, who said, "Ask me for anything but my time."

Yes, our time is precious. But how should we make the best use of it? We all have the same number of minutes in an hour and the same number of hours in a day. So we need to buy opportunities with our time. We need to share our time with someone who needs us.

We usually are glad to give of our skills, our energy, and even our money. But when it comes to giving of our time, . . . well, we're often stingy. Yet nothing is ever accomplished without giving of our time.

Life is short—that's true. But we make it shorter by wasting time. Let's determine not to waste one minute. Let's commit to stop hoarding our hours. Let's not save our time; let's give it away!

Making It Personal

*How can I make the most of what's
left of this day? this week?*

May 13

Joy for the Journey

Don't be dejected and sad, for the joy of the LORD is your strength!
Nehemiah 8:10

Through the years many people have asked me, "Why at your age do you keep on working every day and many weekends, traveling all over, when you could be at home relaxing with your family and enjoying your grandchildren?" My answer to this question is always the same: It is my choice to do this because I love what I do.

That's not to say it's all been a bed of roses. This journey has been long and arduous, the responsibilities sometimes tiring and discouraging. There have been many trials. But at the end of the day, it has always given me joy because I am doing what the Lord wants me to do, and "the joy of the Lord is my strength."

I could never have imagined that I would be taking this path at this time in my life. I never dreamed I would have a purpose so fulfilling. But God knew it! "For I know the plans I have for you, [Joan,] plans for good and not for disaster, to give you a future and a hope" (Jeremiah 29:11). He has planned good things, given me hope and purpose—and joy! And guess what? I still have quality time with my children, grandchildren, and great grandchildren. Isn't God good?

Making It Personal

Does my life exhibit joy and purpose?

The Wonder of It All

*Then I will declare the wonder of your name to my brothers
and sisters. I will praise you among all your people.*
Psalm 22:22

When I think about all that God has done for me throughout my life, I can't help but be filled with wonder and awe at His grace and greatness. The dictionary defines *wonder* as "surprise, astonishment, or admiration; a feeling of amazement; a marvel or a miracle."

The well-known hymn "How Great Thou Art" by Stuart Hine puts this idea of wonder into words:

O Lord my God, when I in awesome wonder,
Consider all the works Thy hands have made.
I see the stars; I hear the mighty thunder,
Thy power throughout the universe displayed.

Then sings my soul,
My Savior God to Thee.
How great Thou art!
How great Thou art!

I pray that we never lose the wonder of it all. It took a miracle to put the stars in place. It took a miracle to hang the world in space. It took a miracle to create each one of us. What a wonder-full God we have!

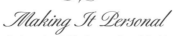

Making It Personal

When was the last time I felt the wonder of God in nature?

A Thankful Heart

I will thank you, LORD, with all my heart;
I will tell of all the marvelous things you have done.
Psalm 9:1

It's not what's in your pocketbook that makes you thankful; it's what is in your heart.

A pastor in Los Angeles visited a shelter for the poor and destitute. He stopped to speak with an elderly lady who was quite cheerful. He asked her how she was doing, and the elderly woman smiled, "I have a great deal to be thankful for—I have two teeth left and they're opposite each other!"

From most people's perspective, this woman really had nothing. But in spite of her circumstances, she found something for which to be thankful. She certainly had the attitude that Paul spoke of in his letter to the Thessalonians, "Always be thankful, for this is God's will for you who belong to Christ Jesus" (1 Thessalonians 5:18). It's what was in her heart, not in her wallet.

Making It Personal

What's in my heart most often—thankfulness or complaining?

Make It Happen

Work brings profit, but mere talk leads to poverty!
Proverbs 14:23 (*Verse of the Year 1989*)

I read a sign at the entrance of a manufacturing plant that read like this: "If you are like a wheelbarrow, going no farther than you are pushed, you need not apply for work here." Some people need to be constantly pushed to accomplish anything worthwhile, don't they? I am sure you know someone like that.

There are three kinds of people: those who make things happen, those who watch things happen, and those who have no idea what has happened! We need to strive to be people who make things happen.

One principle seen through all of the Bible is that work is good. Don't be afraid to dream big and work hard. Take the initiative, get things going, and see them through to completion.

Making It Personal

Am I a "watcher" or a "doer?"

The Sky's the Limit

Humanly speaking, it is impossible. But not with God.
Everything is possible with God.
Mark 10:27

My dear friend Mary Crowley used to say, "I advance in God's potential, not limited by my own." She took that as a theme for her life. We all could. We are not strong enough, smart enough—anything enough—to accomplish much without God's help.

But at the same time, we don't need to limit ourselves by our abilities or perceived lack of ability. When we grab hold of what God's power and potential can do, truly, the sky is the limit. Just think of what we can do with God's potential! It eliminates all the excuses, all the past problems, all the negative history, everything that holds us back. We can perform to our maximum ability and beyond.

I would love to see everyone so convinced of God's potential in and through them that they never say, "I can't do that." Believe that you are not limited by your own potential. Then you can advance in God's potential.

Making It Personal

How will I leave behind my self-imposed limitations today?

Reach the Goal

*Mark out a straight path for your feet;
then stick to the path and stay safe. Don't get sidetracked.*
Proverbs 4:26-27

One of our favorite speakers at our national rallies is Mamie McCullough. In her book *I Can, You Can Too,* Mamie shares her formula for setting goals. I think her advice is fabulous and I've adapted it here. I urge you to personalize it in your life and in your business.

1. *Identify your goals.* (Example: "To contribute to the family income.")
2. *List benefits you will receive from achieving your goals.* ("To be able to pay for a family vacation.")
3. *Set a deadline for achieving your goals.* ("Enough money for a vacation by Memorial Day.")
4. *Identify the major obstacles you will face in reaching your goals.* ("Too shy to put myself forward in business.")
5. *Identify the skills or knowledge required to reach your goals.* ("Ability to speak in front of groups.")
6. *Identify the individuals and/or groups who can help you reach your goals.* ("Boss can coach and encourage me.")
7. *Develop a specific plan of action to reach your goals.* ("Practice public speaking and volunteer for sales presentation at work.")

Once you have identified your plan of action, go for it! Think big and big things will happen.

Making It Personal

What will I include in my goals achievement plan?

Plodding Along

But those who wait on the LORD . . . will walk and not faint.
Isaiah 40:31

How's your business? Is it dragging along behind you? Are you feeling tired and discouraged? God promises we will find new strength—if we confidently trust Him.

Isaiah 40:31 tells us that those who wait on the Lord will walk and not faint. Waiting here means, "to live in confident dependence on the Lord." This is not a passive attitude; it is a positive action of response.

Walking takes effort; to be a plodder is a difficult choice. It's more glamorous and exciting to run. But God said if we trust Him, we will walk and not faint! Isn't that an awesome promise to those who wait on the Lord?

This verse promises new strength. It promises we will not grow weary and we will not faint—in our business, our home, our family.

God cares about your business. But He cares much more about *you*. He will not let you faint, regardless of discouragement, poor health, a difficult supervisor, or few clients. He cares about you and will give you increased strength. Take time to wait—pray, reflect, worship—on the Lord.

Making It Personal

When have I seen God give me strength when I wait on Him?

True Stories

All your words are true; all your just laws will stand forever.
Psalm 119:160

Nine-year-old Danny came bursting out of Sunday school.

"Dad, that story about Moses and all those people crossing the Red Sea was great!" His father smiled and asked the boy to tell him about it.

"Well, the Israelites got out of Egypt, but Pharaoh and his army chased after them. So the Israelites ran as fast as they could until they got to the Red Sea. The Egyptian army was getting closer and closer. So Moses got on his walkie-talkie and told the Israeli Air Force to bomb the Egyptians. While that was happening, the Israeli Navy built a pontoon bridge so the people could cross over. They made it!"

Danny's dad was shocked. "Is that the way they taught you the story?"

"Well, not exactly," Danny admitted. "But if I told you the way they told it to us, you'd never believe it, Dad!"

Some stories we hear *are* too good to be true. But I believe that God's Word is always true.

Making It Personal

What stories in the Bible have inspired me?

Catch and Then Throw

But we must be sure to obey the truth we have learned already.
Philippians 3:16

Just as you need to know the fundamental skills of catching and throwing the ball in baseball, so in your business you need to learn the fundamentals.

Get training whenever possible and learn, learn, learn. Apply, apply, apply. This is catching the ball! Catching the Philosophy and Purpose of Premier Designs is vital. We are a unique company and you need to catch that spirit.

- Our Philosophy—to honor God in all we do
- Our Purpose—to enrich every life we touch
- Our Plan—to serve others through Home Shows

Catch the ball and don't drop it! Then throw the ball to someone willing to catch it. Throwing the ball begins with sharing the Premier story with sincere motives. There are so many lives to enrich. So catch the spirit and then throw that ball.

Making It Personal

How can I share the Premier spirit with someone today?

Adoption

*His unchanging plan has always been to adopt us into
his own family by bringing us to himself through Jesus Christ.*
Ephesians 1:5

I have a good friend who adopted twins, and ever since I have looked at adoption in a whole new way. Several things happen when children are adopted:

1. They receive a new name, the family name.
2. They have to adjust to a new culture.
3. They often have to learn a new language.

When my friend brought her twins home, they were home for good. No probation or trial period. They belonged. That's what God does with us. Through faith in His Son, Jesus, He adopts us as His children, and it's a done deal. We belong. As believers we receive the "family name"— Christian. We become part of a new family culture that marches to the drum of God's Word. We start learning a new language of praise and prayer. What security to know that we belong to God's family.

Making It Personal

What does it mean to me to be adopted into God's family?

Knit Together

*My goal is that they will be encouraged
and knit together by strong ties of love.*
Colossians 2:2

I learned to knit when I was a little girl in Canada. We needed warm sweaters, so I knitted a lot. When you knit, all the stitches need to be accounted for. If one stitch is dropped and not picked up again, a hole forms and it gets larger and larger as you go. One dropped stitch can really affect the entire pattern of the finished product.

This picture of being "knit together in love" is a powerful life illustration. I can just envision a thread of "love" being interwoven, over and under and through our relationships. What a strong pattern that yields.

Think about your close family relationships—any dropped stitches of care there? What about your business colleagues—any loose holes of neglect there? Make an effort to knit your relationships together with love, and pick up any dropped stitches before they are lost.

Making It Personal

Where am I dropping stitches of love in my relationships?

The Power of Family

So commit yourselves completely to these words of mine. . . . Teach them to your children. Talk about them when you are at home and when you are away.
Deuteronomy 11:18-19

What is a family? Strictly speaking it is "a household, a social unit consisting of parents and the children that they rear." But we all know it's much more than that rather scientific definition.

Edith Schaeffer, wife of author and theologian Francis Schaeffer, wrote a book several years ago entitled *What Is a Family?* I like her description of family: "A family is an ever-changing life mobile, a formation center for human relationships, a perpetual relay of truth and a museum of memories."

We all learn how to view the world, how to love and relate, how to deal with conflict—or not—in our families of origin. For some people, early family memories may not be good ones. For others family times were sweet. Whatever our background, we can always be thankful, knowing that God uses everything in our lives for good.

Forming loving relationships, passing on wisdom and truth, making good memories. Make these your family goals today.

Making It Personal

What do I appreciate about my family relationships?

Think on These Things

Whatever is true, whatever is noble, whatever is right, whatever is pure,
whatever is lovely, whatever is admirable—
if anything is excellent or praiseworthy—think about such things.
Philippians 4:8 (NIV)

What we think about influences us more than we know. The Bible tells us to think about all the good things God has given us in the world. Take some time to think about what is:

- *True*—I will not "shade" any of my thoughts with deceit or lies.
- *Noble or good*—I am going to think about others with respect and honor.
- *Right*—I determine to think on what is virtuous and decent.
- *Pure*—I will keep my thoughts focused on good things.
- *Lovely*—I will look for that inner beauty in the people I meet. I will thank God for all the beauty He created.
- *Admirable*—I will focus on the best qualities of people I know and respect.
- *Excellent*—I will avoid shortcuts and sloppy attitudes.
- *Praiseworthy*—I will recall those things that cause my heart to praise God.

Compare your thoughts, actions, and words to this checklist during the hectic times as well as the quiet times.

Making It Personal

Do I need to do some housecleaning of my thoughts?

Get in Shape

Physical exercise has some value, but spiritual exercise is much more important, for it promises a reward in both this life and the next.
1 Timothy 4:8

We live in a health-conscious society. Listen in on any conversation, and if we wait long enough, it will turn to the subject of dieting, new recipes, or exercise of some kind. Healthy food, regular exercise, and rest are generally accepted to be the basic building blocks of good physical health. Let's apply this "healthy trinity" to our inner, spiritual lives as well.

We are to "crave pure spiritual milk" (1 Peter 2:2). A daily drink of God's Word nourishes our faith.

Secondly, regular spiritual exercise yields rewards now and eternally (1 Timothy 4:8). Stretch those muscles of faith by applying the principles of God's Word.

Finally, regarding rest, David wrote in one of his psalms, "Oh, how I wish I had wings like a dove; then I would fly away and rest!" (Psalm 55:6). I could write, "Oh, how I wish for a cruise so I could sail away and rest!" We must take time for renewing our souls spiritually by being still in God's presence.

Food, exercise, and rest all add up to a spiritually dynamic, successful, and healthy person. Let's get in shape!

Making It Personal

What can I do to have a healthier spiritual life?

A Magnetic Personality

You must have the qualities of salt among yourselves
and live in peace with each other.
Mark 9:50

What is this thing called *personality?* It is all the qualities that form an individual's character. It's you, the real you that people come to know and like (or dislike). It's the part of you that makes an impression on other people.

Everyone has heard about a magnetic personality. A magnet attracts and draws something to itself. People who attract us are:

- sincere and not fake
- friendly to everyone
- interested in people
- considerate and thoughtful
- of pleasant countenance (they smile a lot!)
- appreciative of others
- enthusiastic
- optimistic
- consistent (not moody)

Each one of these magnetic characteristics is related to how we interact with others. We can't avoid living with people, so it's important that we learn how to get along with them.

Making It Personal

Which one of these characteristics do I need to cultivate more?

Living with Virtue

*"Can anyone hide from me? Am I not everywhere in all
the heavens and earth?" asks the LORD.*
Jeremiah 23:24

Aristotle wrote, "If you would understand virtue,
observe the conduct of virtuous men" (and of
women too!).

The number of political skeletons that have come out
of closets these past few years in our nation's capital are
just the tip of the iceberg of the millions of undiscovered
cheatings, evasions, cover-ups, and half-truths in the whole
of society. "Everybody does it" seems to be the slogan for
our times.

Some people think, *What does it matter if I hedge a little
on the expense sheet?* Or *Who cares if I bend my wedding vows
just once?* Or *No one will ever know if I take a few supplies from
the office.*

But God knows, and we must live to honor Him.
Integrity and virtue begin at home. Women of virtue live
with honesty and integrity, whether someone's watching or
not. We must be careful how we live behind the scenes as
well as in the spotlight.

Making It Personal

What difference does it make to me that I cannot hide from God?

Choosing to Trust

But don't be angry with yourselves that you did this to me, for God did it.
He sent me here ahead of you to preserve your lives.
Genesis 45:5

I love the story of Joseph. It's an amazing tale of high drama and forgiveness. (You can read his story in the book of Genesis, chapters 37, 39–50.)

Joseph's life was a stark contrast to his father Jacob's life. While Jacob was a schemer, Joseph was a dreamer. Joseph had several dreams as a young man, showing his brothers bowing down to him. This did not make him popular. He was also his father's favorite. His brothers hated him enough to sell him into slavery.

In Egypt, Joseph experienced all sorts of persecution and setbacks, but he always knew that God was with him. And when his brothers came to Egypt for food, he welcomed them with open arms.

Joseph chose to forget the awful details of his long journey, choosing instead to put his complete trust in God's plan for his life. While Jacob wrestled with God, Joseph trusted God.

Making It Personal

Do I cling to the hard stuff in my life, or trust God with it?

Forgiveness Works

*Then Joseph kissed each of his brothers and wept over them,
and then they began talking freely with him.*
Genesis 45:15

If you've looked at Joseph's story, you know that his family was one of the original dysfunctional families! He suffered a deep betrayal at the hand of his own brothers. Yet later, he flourished as a leader. There are many lessons we can take away from Joseph's life.

1. Showing favoritism has consequences. Joseph's father was overly partial to this son, and it was the root of major problems in their family. Treat each member of your family with the same love and respect. Favoritism will gnaw away at the unity of your home.

2. Be forgiving. When Joseph finally revealed his identity to the brothers, he chose not to blame them for what they had done to him. He forgave. Forgiveness brings freedom.

3. Trust God. Joseph chose to live for God and not for himself. We can choose the same.

Making It Personal

What can I take away from Joseph's example?

Remembering on Memorial Day

Praise the LORD, I tell myself, and never forget the good things he does for me.
Psalm 103:2

Memory is a wonderful gift. We store away all kinds of wonderful events from the past in our memory bank. We also have some sad recollections.

Psychologists tell us that our memory is not so much a storehouse that we empty and fill as we desire; rather, it is a process by which we rehearse past experiences. And yet even important things gradually fade away from our memory. That's one reason why we have set aside days such as Memorial Day. These holidays are memory aids so we won't forget some important things.

It's so easy to forget all the veterans who gave their lives so we can enjoy freedom. We forget how much we owe to our country. Even more tragically, we forget how much we owe to God for allowing us to live here with freedom. A forgetful heart soon becomes a foolish heart. The one who forgets God is in as great a danger as the one who forgets that a red light means we must stop.

I hope we can make this Memorial Day a day of remembering those who have sacrificed for our freedom, but most of all remembering God and His blessings.

Making It Personal

How can I thank and honor the war veterans I know?

June

God's ways are always good and always purposeful.

With love,
Joan

June 1

Temperature Change

*Love each other with genuine affection, and take
delight in honoring each other.*
Romans 12:10

My pastor, W. A. Criswell, always preached wonderful
sermons. One time he stated, "What was the
difference between the waves upon which the *Titanic*
floated safely and the iceberg that sank the great ship?
Both waves and ice were made of the same thing; the only
difference was the temperature!"

In your business and in your relationships you can
float or sink by the "temperature" you present. Are you
keeping it personal? You can make a huge difference by
relating with warmth and genuine interest.

Relationships are so very important. We want everyone to feel important, because we believe everyone is
somebody! Plan that personal touch.

Making It Personal
With what "temperature" do I relate to others?

Wisdom in Real Life

If you need wisdom—if you want to know what God wants you to do—ask him, and he will gladly tell you. He will not resent your asking.
James 1:5

I have lived through many experiences in which I've needed wisdom. One situation in particular was not fun in the middle of the process. I was ill and the doctor told us, "We may never know what has caused your illness." After a week of tests, it turned out he was right; they did not know anything more.

Because of this, we had to make some decisions about some commitments we had made. We had the facts, we prayed and asked for wisdom, we added in our common sense, and made the hard decision to cancel some things. It saddened me that I couldn't go on a special cruise with our Premier people nor spend time in Argentina with special missionary friends.

But you know what? While I was recuperating, God used that quiet time at home to work in my life and in Andy's life (and you know he would never sit still that long unless he had to!). During that time God gave us marvelous direction for a new focus in our business. A double dose of wisdom came from a tough situation. It's exciting to have God in your life!

Making It Personal
For what situation do I need wisdom today?

Return to Service

*Let your good deeds shine out for all to see, so that
everyone will praise your heavenly Father.*
Matthew 5:16

We are told we live in a "service economy," but
have you noticed how that service economy really
works?

You drive to a service station (which is now called a
"convenience center") so you can pump your own gas,
check your own oil, wash your own windshield, and get
your own coffee. Then you go to the bank, where you
make your own deposit and withdraw your own money.
Finally, you go to a fast-food restaurant, where you go to
the counter to place your order, carry your own tray to your
table (which may or may not be clean), and get your own
napkins and plasticware. On the way out, you are asked to
clean off the table and put your trash in a container.

Let's put the service back in the "service economy"—
and glorify our heavenly Father by letting our good deeds
shine.

Making It Personal

How can I let my light of good deeds shine out today?

Burn Those Bridges

Victory comes from you, O LORD.
May your blessings rest on your people.
Psalm 3:8

In Texas, we consider the Alamo in San Antonio a sacred place in history. After General Santa Ana defeated the Texas forces there at the Alamo, he pursued the troops under the command of Sam Houston. Houston's force was badly outnumbered and was easily backed up against the San Jacinto River. He was essentially cut off by the huge numbers led by Santa Ana.

Houston called for his faithful orderly and commanded him to burn the bridge behind them, which crossed the San Jacinto River. The orderly responded by reminding Houston that it was the only way out. Houston replied, "Burn the bridge! That is not the way we are going out of here." The bridge was burned and, of course, history records the total defeat of the Mexican Army by General Houston and his troops.

Do you have a bridge to burn? Are there habits or unresolved conflicts that need to be burned up? Do you and I need to confess our sins of unforgiveness? Today is a great day to burn our bridges, with no retreat available. We can claim a victory just as General Sam Houston did.

Making It Personal

What bridges do I need to burn to experience more freedom and victory in my life?

Committed to Lead

Now that my servant Moses is dead, you must lead my people across the Jordan River into the land I am giving them.
Joshua 1:2

In the Old Testament, we read about Joshua, one of the most extraordinary leaders in the Bible. Joshua had been Moses' personal attendant throughout the forty years the children of Israel wandered in the wilderness.

After Moses died, the mantle of leadership fell to Joshua. God told Joshua to lead the people in to conquer the Promised Land, a rather daunting task. He had already put his time in, hadn't he? Wasn't it time for someone else to lead? But Joshua was committed to God, he was committed to God's people, and he was committed to the goal. So he stayed and obeyed.

Were there setbacks as they faced countless enemies? Of course. Were there headaches? Of course. Did everyone eagerly follow Joshua's lead? Of course not. But his commitment to God was sure, "As for me and my family, we will serve the Lord" (Joshua 24:15).

One thing we learn from Joshua is this: Leadership without commitment is no leadership at all. Choose to lead and serve well, no matter what role you find yourself in right now.

Making It Personal

What would it look like to lead well in my spheres of influence right now, whether in my business or at home?

Keep the Standard

Be strong and very courageous. Obey all the laws Moses gave you. Do not turn away from them, and you will be successful in everything you do.
Joshua 1:7

Joshua took on a huge job after his mentor, Moses, died. Was Joshua's decision to lead just a blind stab in the dark? No. He had watched Moses in action and seen him deal with difficult situations. He had been trained in the commandments and laws. Then he practiced that commitment after Moses was gone and passed on the same teaching.

To be an effective leader you must be committed to the right things and live that commitment out in your life. Always keep in mind the moral standards of your business and then train others with those same standards.

Our company's commitment to its Philosophy and Purpose and Plan has not changed: to honor God and enrich lives. Are you committed to that? Do you think Joshua changed plans in midstream as the mood hit him, or was he committed to God's plan as taught him by Moses?

What we can learn from Joshua is summed up in an anonymous statement I once read: "Leadership without personal commitment to an unchanging standard leads to moral corruption, unethical behavior, and erosion."

Making It Personal

What is the standard I'm following as I lead others?

Keeping My Balance

I am overwhelmed, and you alone know the way I should turn.
Psalm 142:3

Remember the teeter-totter? (Or the see-saw, as I called it when I was little.) A teeter-totter needs to have about the same weight on each end in order for it to be any fun. If one side is too heavy, you can't go up and down. Unbalanced, the teeter-totter will crash on one side while the other is left high and dry!

Sometimes I feel like I'm on that teeter-totter in my life, teetering one way, then tottering the other way. We all need to find a good balance between work and play, between quiet time alone and time with others, between work and family relationships. Too much of either side takes a toll, and we can become overwhelmed and crash.

I believe that there is an enemy of our souls, who is pushing us one way and then the other. He loves to see us struggle to maintain balance in our home and work lives. But you can keep from falling prey to his lies if you take the time to clarify your values and ask God to give you wisdom. Change is possible if you seek God's help.

Making It Personal

What parts of my life are out of balance?

Teamwork

The body has many different parts, not just one part.
1 Corinthians 12:14

A baseball team has many players from different countries, but they play together to win their game. An orchestra has many different instruments, and they don't always play the same notes, but the music sounds beautiful. Similarly, the apostle Paul used the analogy of the human body to describe the diversity-in-unity of the Christian church.

Relationships also require teamwork. Marriages require the cooperation of both the husband and the wife. Family life depends upon the cooperation of parents and children.

It is the same in business. In a company, everyone has different skills and abilities, but each one is important to the success of the enterprise. We are all different parts, but together we are one! Work together with the other members of your team to serve each other and your customers, and to make the company the very best it can be.

Making It Personal

How can I become a better team player?

June 9

The Two "D's"

Get the truth and don't ever sell it;
also get wisdom, discipline, and discernment.
Proverbs 23:23

The book of Proverbs challenges us to get wisdom. Part of wisdom is discipline. Self-discipline is difficult, especially for certain sanguine personalities that make up a lot of sales companies. Proverbs 23:23 lists four goals to have: truth, wisdom, discipline, and discernment, or understanding. They are all interrelated.

Let's look at some things that require self-discipline. We must be disciplined to have integrity. We must be disciplined with our tongues to speak truth and refrain from gossip. We must be disciplined to regularly train ourselves and those in our business. Discipline says you have endurance and don't give up.

Another aspect of wisdom is discernment, or understanding. Here's a simple formula that may help you become more understanding. I call it the "Feel, Felt, Found Theory."

- *I understand how you feel.*
- *I once felt that way.*
- *But I found that by doing this . . . I could overcome.*

King Solomon said, "Let those who are wise listen to these proverbs and become even wiser" (Proverbs 1:5). That is great advice, isn't it? If you are wise, become wiser.

Making It Personal

In which area do I need to grow more: discipline or discernment?

Adding Up Time

Redeeming the time, because the days are evil.
Ephesians 5:16 (NKJV)

We all have the same amount of time. Seven days, 168 hours, in every week. I believe a true leader can never say, "I don't have the time." Very seldom is that strictly true. The problem is not in needing more time, but of making better use of the time we have. Let's look at how a week's time pans out.

One day a week should be a day of rest. God ordained that. That leaves six days to work at your job and take care of your family. Now, do the math:

6 days x 24 hours = 144 hours left.

6 nights x 8 hours for sleep = 48 hours off that.

That leaves 96 hours remaining to divide between family and work.

Let's cut that in two, say 40 hours a week for work, which is reasonable. Leaving 40-50 hours for family and other.

However you add, multiply, subtract, or divide it, I think you will be pleasantly surprised to find more hours available than you may have thought you had! Make the most of it.

Making It Personal

What am I spending my time on?

Personal Keystrokes

And everything you do must be done with love.
1 Corinthians 16:14

Technology today is wonderful for complex business systems. We often wonder how we were able to keep accounting records before, or how we ever kept inventory straight. But there are downsides to being dependent on technology, too.

Once we were stuck in an airport for hours and hours when a computer glitch caused 800 flights to be cancelled. Another time, the airline computers at an airport were all shut down due to no electricity. No flights could come in or go out, and there was nothing they could do about it. No personal touch could relieve the situation.

Another downside is a loss of real relationships with a human touch. I agree that e-mails are acceptable in a business environment, but e-mails do not usually build personal relationships. To be honest, I rarely feel "warmed" by e-mails I receive. The words in that format just don't feel personal. Even the attempt to write a "smiley face" is sideways, and to me that is not personal.

One way to combat losing the human touch is by picking up a pen once in a while. I have long encouraged writing handwritten notes. There is such a friendly, heartwarming feel when you read handwritten words, instead of keystrokes.

Making It Personal

Is technology ruling me or am I ruling my technology?

How Do You Spell Leadership?

If God has given you leadership ability, take the responsibility seriously.
Romans 12:8

Jim Miller, of Miller Business Systems, provided the following acrostic on leadership in his book entitled *The Corporate Coach*. I have "Hornerized" it.

If you are heading up any kind of team, then you are a leader. A good leader must have the following traits and abilities.

L is for *listening*. Be a good listener and have an open mind as you make yourself available for your team members.

E is for *enabling*. Get others to play on the team too.

A is for *ambition*. Set goals and work to achieve them.

D is for *desire*. Show enthusiasm.

E is for *example*. Serve as a role model.

R is for *respect*. Show respect for others and build up their self-esteem.

S is for *self-esteem*. Believe in yourself.

H is for *heart*. Empathize and encourage others.

I is for *initiative*. Make things happen.

P is for *patience*. Be quick to praise but slow to criticize.

Making It Personal

Which of these leadership traits do I need to cultivate most?

On Display

*For the Scriptures say that God told Pharaoh, "I have appointed you
for the very purpose of displaying my power in you, and so that
my fame might spread throughout the earth."*
Romans 9:17

The powerful Pharaoh in ancient Egypt was a study
in stubborn arrogance. When Moses told him to let
God's people leave their enslavement, Pharaoh contested
him time after time. Along with Pharaoh's own pride
and stubbornness, the Bible says that God "hardened
his heart." Why? There's no rhyme or reason to that, we
might think.

But God's ways are always purposeful. He said, "I
will cause Pharaoh to be stubborn *so I can multiply my
miraculous signs and wonders* in the land of Egypt. . . . And
the Egyptians will know that I am the LORD!" (Exodus
7:3; 14:4). God used all of that for a higher purpose:
to display His awesome power and so His name would
be glorified.

When hard things happen in our lives, it may seem
that there is no rhyme or reason to it. But God's ways are
always good. Depend on it. Look to see how His purpose
and power can be displayed in your life.

Making It Personal

What is my life displaying: my power or God's power?

Something to Celebrate

Whatever is good and perfect comes to us from God above, who created all heaven's lights. Unlike them, he never changes or casts shifting shadows.
James 1:17

Celebrate: to observe or commemorate an event with ceremonies or festivities; to make known publicly. That's how the dictionary defines what it means to celebrate. (I like to add in "observe a special event with *gifts!*")

Sometimes we prefer to have private celebrations and that has its place. But remember what celebrating really means: to joyfully observe something and make it known. That implies letting others in on the good news.

When I think about all the blessings I enjoy—our wonderful country and the freedoms we enjoy, my family, health, good friends, having work that I enjoy—I have to celebrate publicly. James 1:17 tells us, "Whatever is good and perfect comes to us from God above, who created all heaven's lights." God is the source of all good gifts. And so I celebrate! I want to rejoice and let everyone know how thankful I am for God's good gifts.

Making It Personal

What is on my list of good gifts that I can celebrate and make known today?

Something Special

His unchanging plan has always been to adopt us into his own family by bringing us to himself through Jesus Christ. And this gave him great pleasure.
Ephesians 1:5

Have you ever wondered if God has feelings? He is so powerful and almighty and so "other," that it's hard to imagine God with feelings. But the Bible talks about something that gives God pleasure—His children! "His unchanging plan has always been to adopt us into his own family. . . . And this gave him great pleasure" (Ephesians 1:5). His pleasure is not dependent on us, of course. But He chooses to relate to us and that somehow brings him joy.

God knows all my faults; He knows the *real* me. And I still give Him great pleasure because He adopted me into His family. To think that God knew me before I was born and that He chose me before the world was created. Isn't that an awesome thought? That ought to make me feel special. What about you?

Making It Personal

Do I believe I'm special to God? Why or why not?

Our Heavenly Daddy

For all who are led by the Spirit of God are children of God . . .
adopted into his family—calling him "Father, dear Father."
Romans 8:14-15

As we think about Father's Day, I like to reflect on God's qualities as our heavenly Father. Romans 8:14-15 clearly tells me that if we are His children, we can call Him "Father." The original word used here was *Abba*, which literally means "Daddy."

This is so personal! God is my own Father, my Daddy, who tells me in His "personal note" to me (the Bible, His Word) that "I have loved you with an everlasting love" (Jeremiah 31:3). Now, how long is everlasting? It never ends! He loves me even when I am unlovely, disobedient, and just plain tacky. My heavenly Father is never sarcastic. He never gives me the silent treatment. He never withdraws His love. That's His personal fatherly touch.

Some of us have had good dads, and some have had not so good dads. No earthly father is perfect. But our heavenly Father is perfect, loves us completely, and will never leave us.

Making It Personal

Do I view God as my "Father"? If not, why not?

Go for the Gold

I discipline my body like an athlete, training it to do what it should.
1 Corinthians 9:27

When athletes are going for the gold, they get in shape. Katarina Witt didn't win the gold medal in figure skating on her dreams and good looks alone. She was in good condition. It took hours and hours of practice and vigorous training to achieve her goals and win.

What about your business? Do you have desires and goals to achieve? One way to get in shape in order to reach those goals is to take advantage of all the learning opportunities there are. We should all be continual students. We can always learn something new that will help us grow.

Don't try to do everything you learn all at once. Be patient, stay in shape, and press on. You must be consistent if you want to reach that goal. So go for the gold and never give up!

Making It Personal

What new training do I need to achieve my goals?

Hidden Blessing

If you serve Christ with this attitude, you will please God.
And other people will approve of you, too.
Romans 14:18

A man was hiking and came to a mountain pass. It was late in autumn and snow was beginning to fall as the man climbed the steep slopes. The trail was long, and the man was freezing.

After great difficulty, he reached the top. There he found a stranger lying on the ground, unconscious and near death from the bitter cold. Forgetting his own discomfort, the man hurried to the suffering stranger and began to massage his body and limbs vigorously.

Before long, the stranger showed signs of life. After brisk exercising, the stranger was restored to full consciousness. The amazing thing the man discovered was that by working hard to save the stranger's life, he himself had become warm and strong again. After returning to safety, the two men became fast friends.

Which man received the greater blessing? I think they both did. Take time to care, to walk alongside someone, to be a friend. That is all part of the blessing of serving.

Making It Personal

When have I been blessed by serving someone else?

Coming Alongside

Older women must train the younger women.
Titus 2:4

I have a burden for mothers who have young children and a thriving home business to balance each day. I know it is frustrating to many of them, and my heart goes out to them. There are so many negative influences on family life. They need encouragement and help to know how to deal with all the ups and downs.

The Bible teaches that we have an enemy of our souls, and the devil would like nothing more than to attack us where we are most vulnerable—in our homes and in our jobs. Especially when our jobs enrich lives and serve others! He will do all he can to disrupt families, discourage young moms, and break up a business that is honoring God. We must be vigilant.

Older women must be available to come alongside younger women, and to help with this balancing act. Let them know it is possible because many of us have done it! Let's be ready to help where and when we can.

Making It Personal

Am I available to lend a helping hand to a busy mom?

Summer Joy

*Don't let the excitement of youth cause you to forget your Creator. Honor him
in your youth before you grow old and no longer enjoy living.*
Ecclesiastes 12:1

When our children were growing up, I loved the months of summer when the kids were out of school. We had great family togetherness. We went camping and swimming. We had time for Bible study together in the mornings, and my sons had ball games in the evenings. We were active and energetic, with seemingly no responsibilities. Those were the days.

Queen Esther is an example of a woman who was active, too. When she became Queen of Persia she was probably no older than twenty years old. She was in the "summer" of her life. As a woman of influence, she used her position responsibly to save her people, the Jews, from a plot of destruction. She did all this in the young summer season of her life.

No matter what age or season we are in, God has given us responsibilities and challenges we need to meet. Sometimes we like to make excuses for not being responsible during our early summer years. But as a young woman Esther used her influence for good; can we do less?

Making It Personal

What am I facing today that requires an active response?

Get Creative

For we are God's masterpiece. He has created us anew in Christ Jesus,
so that we can do the good things he planned for us long ago.
Ephesians 2:10

When we hear the word "creative" we often think of musicians, poets, and artistic geniuses. But good leaders also show a measure of *creativity*.

We are all born with some creativity, but I think it gets lost along the way. We must restore our sense of wonder and awe, not only in the natural world around us but also in the business environment in which we find ourselves. Truly creative people are dedicated to their craft. They think for themselves and look at things in a fresh and new way.

Our example of how to live creatively is Jesus Christ. He had complete integrity. He was dedicated to His mission. He related to situations in new and fresh ways. And He certainly was creative in His teaching methods, asking penetrating questions and telling wonderful parables to make His points. Follow His example and get creative!

Making It Personal

How creative am I in my work these days?

Knowledge that Counts

*Let them boast in this alone: that they truly know me
and understand that I am the LORD.*
Jeremiah 9:24

A uthor Robert Stone observed "There is more information available than there are things to know." I
certainly agree. I once read that if new scientific information
continues to accumulate at its present rate, and if it was all
published in a scientific journal, the journal would weigh
more than the earth by the year 2020! I don't know if that's
really accurate, but it's something to think about.

We are fairly drowning in information. No lack there.
What we lack is real knowledge—true spiritual knowledge.
God says the only knowledge that counts eternally is
knowing Him. And if we had ten lifetimes, we could never
get to the bottom of that subject. Take some time today to
seek after God, who is the Source of all knowledge.

Making It Personal

How can I gain more of the knowledge that counts?

Family Values

You should be like one big happy family, full of sympathy toward each other, loving one another with tender hearts and humble minds.
1 Peter 3:8 (TLB) (Verse of the Year 1988)

A family can mean different things nowadays. It can be two parents and their children. It can be one parent and children. It can be grandparents raising grandchildren.

But any way you put it, a family is any blend of people designed for the growth of those within that family unit. It is an important center for developing physically, mentally, and emotionally. It is there we gain the valuable things in life—memories, beliefs, and attitudes. The family prepares children for life, laying the foundation for their moral character.

The family is society's most important institution. Many times we overlook or underestimate its importance. If the family fails, all the other institutions of society will also fail. We must work hard at building loving families. Nothing strengthens loyalty in a family more than love. It breaks down internal competition, builds morale, and says, "I belong."

You have heard it said, "Houses are made of wood and stone, but only love can make a home." That's a good recipe for building a big happy family.

Making It Personal

What is the love quotient in my family right now?

Look and Listen

Anyone who is willing to hear should listen and understand.
Matthew 13:9

One of my special memories is when I met George W. Bush. My son Tim and I were selecting a suite at the new Arlington ballpark. Mr. Bush was the Texas Rangers owner then, and he spent time with us helping us make a good decision. During our conversation, he never took his eyes off of us when he spoke to us. His attention was a very important part of listening.

You can have all the wisdom in the world, but until the other person believes you have listened and heard them, your words of advice will fall on deaf ears. So listen to those who train you. Listen to your colleagues and customers. Listen to your spouse and children. And always listen to that still small voice of God. If we do, we will all be better people and better businesswomen.

Making It Personal

Why is it so hard to really listen sometimes?

A Body of Many Parts

There are many parts, but only one body.
The eye can never say to the hand, "I don't need you."
1 Corinthians 12:20-21

I once had an arthritic joint in my hand wear out. The rest of my hand and arm was healthy and strong, but with that weak joint, I couldn't do much. Then I had the joint replaced, and my hand could fully function again. I learned that my little hand joint was just as important as my big arm bone—all parts are necessary.

The Bible says, "The body has many different parts. . . . Suppose the whole body were an eye—then how would you hear? Or if your whole body were just one big ear, how could you smell anything? But God made our bodies with many parts, and he has put each part just where he wants it" (1 Corinthians 12:14-18).

How does that apply to businesswomen? In every way! What if your company had nothing but salespeople; who would manage the company? What if everyone were accountants; who would type letters? We are uniquely designed to complete the whole picture and each part is necessary.

Remember that you are important to your business, and so is everyone with whom you work.

Making It Personal

How can I treat everyone in my business,
including myself, as important?

Be a "Grandmother"

Children are a gift from the LORD; they are a reward from him.
Psalm 127:3

I have fourteen grandchildren, and it's great to be a grandmother! Our grandchildren are truly gifts from the Lord—precious souls, each one of them.

But one thing I have learned from observing my grandchildren with their mothers, as well as from being a mother myself, is that children are terribly dependent upon Mom. Especially when children are very young, mothers are interrupted night and day to meet their needs. That's why, as a grandmother, I enjoy helping out in small ways.

This is a vivid illustration of what you should be doing for the "children" or "grandchildren" in your business. When new people join the work family, they are special somebodys, aren't they? But they are also dependent upon you and other established members of the company for encouragement. Help new Jewelers put down strong roots and nurture them as much as you can.

Do a deed by simple kindness,
Though its end you may not see,
It may reach like widening ripples,
Down a long eternity.

Making It Personal

What deed of kindness can I do for a new colleague this week?

Time to Plant

There is a time for everything, a season for every activity under heaven . . . A time to plant and a time to harvest.
Ecclesiastes 3:1-2

A time for everything and a season for every activity— what a great thought! But does that mean I can do *whatever* I wish *whenever* I wish? No, I don't believe it does.

God has set boundaries on time. A season is not forever; it is a prescribed amount of time. With that in mind, let's consider what Ecclesiastes might mean for you when it says, "A time to plant and a time to harvest" (verse 2).

In your work life and your family life right now, are you planting or are you harvesting? If you are planting, maybe you are spreading the word about your business or launching a new product. If you are a mother, maybe you are planting love, morals, and values in the hearts of your children.

Maybe your time of planting has progressed to harvest time. Maybe you are expanding your business or reaping financial rewards for work done earlier. At home, you may be enjoying the effects of training you have given your kids. What an exciting time!

Planting and harvesting are both hard work, but God honors hard work. Are you ready?

Making It Personal

What should I be planting or harvesting right now?

What's Your Hurry?

*Be patient with each other, making allowance for
each other's faults because of your love.*
Ephesians 4:2

Have you noticed that we Americans are not a patient
people? "I want patience and I want it now!" the
saying goes. I have seen many near accidents as drivers
went through an intersection when a caution light was
blinking—sometimes they even went through a red light!
Have you been in line at the grocery store checkout and
changed lines just to get out two seconds sooner? What is
our hurry?

The Bible has great instructions for us regarding patience.
For instance, Proverbs 25:15 says, "Patience can persuade a
prince." Wow! I haven't dealt with a prince lately, but that is
good advice in case I meet one soon. Seriously, that verse is
telling us that patience is a valuable trait to have.

- Be patient when Jenny Jeweler calls at 6:30 P.M.,
  saying she can't take care of the training tonight.
- Be patient when Cathy Customer decides she doesn't
  like the product she bought and wants to return it.
- Be patient when Nancy Neighbor cancels her Home
  Show two hours before it's supposed to start.

As Ephesians 4:2 tells us, we are to make allowances for
others because of our love.

Making It Personal

How can I make allowances for others today?

June 29

Goodbye, Comfort Zone

*Do not be afraid or discouraged. For the LORD
your God is with you wherever you go.*
Joshua 1:9

Most human beings like to be comfortable, free from burdens, worries, and risks. It's normal to want to play it safe. But playing it safe isn't always the best thing. I think many of us wrestle with getting out of our comfort zones and growing in ways we need to grow.

Someone sent me an anonymous poem about just this idea. Here are a few lines of it to reflect on.

> *I used to have a comfort zone*
> *where I knew I couldn't fail.*
> *The same four walls and busy work*
> *were really more like jail. . . .*
>
> *I claimed to be so busy*
> *with things inside the zone.*
> *But deep inside I longed*
> *for something special of my own. . . .*
>
> *I took a step and, with new strength*
> *I'd never felt before,*
> *I kissed my comfort zone goodbye*
> *and closed and locked the door.*

Making It Personal

What is my comfort zone? What first step can I take outside of it?

Tranquila in My Spirit

I will praise the LORD at all times. I will constantly speak his praises.
Psalm 34:1

In February 1994, I lay in a hospital bed in Caracas, Venezuela, struggling to breathe. My physician, Dr. Carmen, would come by my bed, take my hand in hers, and say, *"Tranquila, tranquila,* Joan." "Peace, peace." How could I tell her that I was *tranquila* in my spirit? Outside, illness and disease were raging, but I knew my heavenly Father was with me, and He gave me calmness.

My friend Tom Hemingway had reminded me just three days before I went to Venezuela that God is never surprised. Whatever we go through, He has already been there. I believed that, and so I praised the Lord and had peace.

During my illness, I put some faith in my doctors as they ministered to me in the hospital for eighteen days. But ultimately I was in God's hands. I share this with you so that you can give thanks to God for all He has done in your life, even during dark and dreary days. To Him be all praise and honor!

Making It Personal

What will I praise God for this day?

July

How very blessed we are to be Americans! Take time today to remember God's blessings.

With love,
Joan

Keeping It Personal in Relationships

There are "friends" who destroy each other,
but a real friend sticks closer than a brother.
Proverbs 18:24

How are you doing at building personal relationships? *Webster's Dictionary* defines the word *personal* to mean "peculiar to a certain person, individual; done in person." The term *relationship* is defined as "the relation that connects or binds participants." Underneath all that we do, "keeping it personal" means *having relationships*, connecting, building friendships, and giving of ourselves to others.

Relationships are things women generally do well. We all know people who have more friends than you can shake a stick at. But there are different levels of friendship. We can't have a hundred "best friends." And deeper friendships don't just happen by chance. We have to work at them. Relationships take a huge interest to begin, and after they begin, they require high maintenance. We must value that personal relationship and spend time developing it.

So don't wait. Start "keeping it personal" in your relationships and make a new friend.

Making It Personal

How can I deepen a friendship with someone today?

Carry Your Torch

*We want each of you to show this same diligence to
the very end, in order to make your hope sure.*
Hebrews 6:11 (NIV)

The Olympic Torch represents honorable competition among athletes striving for the gold medal. When Andy had the honor of carrying the Olympic Torch on its journey across America to Salt Lake City, he was part of a team of over 11,000 people who walked, ran, used wheelchairs, and canes. They all had one goal: to pass on that torch and to keep that light brightly burning.

What if one of the torchbearers decided it was just too cold to continue? Or perhaps a person in a wheelchair couldn't get across a bridge that was closed for repairs. What if Andy had been distracted by all the people cheering and stopped to visit with everyone? (Not exactly out of the question for him!) The 2002 Olympics could not have begun if any of these scenarios had played out.

Sometimes we can feel as if our life is at a stopping place. Perhaps you have become sidetracked by distractions or busyness. You have stopped growing; you have stopped carrying the "torch" for whatever reason. Each one of us is carrying a torch of service, of hope, of opportunity. Hebrews 6:11 encourages us to be diligent to the end.

Making It Personal

What is keeping me from diligently carrying my torch of hope?

Time to Remember

Then at last his people believed his promises. Then they finally sang his praise. Yet how quickly they forgot what he had done!
Psalm 106:12-13

Today is a good time to remember what God has done for us as a nation and as individuals. I don't know about you, but I am guilty of staying pretty close to God in times of crisis. But when things are going smoothly, I go on my independent way. Well, it looks like the Hebrew people in the Old Testament had the same lifestyle. Forgetfulness was a problem.

What a powerful three-line description is given of God's people in Psalm 106:12-13: (1) they believed God's promises; (2) they sang God's praises; and (3) they soon forgot what God had done!

If there is any description of America today, this is it. We don't need to depend upon God for much of anything. He has blessed America abundantly. We have our daily bread. We have freedom in our country, and are the envy of the world. We have had the incomparable privilege as a nation to help other nations with food and assistance. How very blessed we are—yet how quickly we forget all that God has done for us. Take time today to remember God's blessings.

Making It Personal

What is one blessing for which I am grateful today?

July 4

America the Beautiful

Then if my people who are called by my name will humble themselves and pray ... I will hear from heaven and will forgive their sins and heal their land.
2 Chronicles 7:14

As we celebrate America's Independence Day, I am so grateful to be an American. We live in the greatest country in the world. Yet in many ways we are facing a crisis as a nation—a moral crisis. America is not united. Our country seems to be divided in half—not north and south, east and west—but the dividing line is a political one in all directions.

When we moved to this country in 1950, America was a different nation. God has blessed our country unbelievably. But little by little our values and morals are eroding. Malls and stores are open all day on Sunday. Prayer is not allowed in schools. Abortion is on the rise; babies murdered by the millions. I won't list all the sins—you know about them well. In the half a century we have lived in America, I have never seen the out-and-out hatred in the political arena that we witness today. It is a spiritual struggle we are watching—evil against good; faith against unbelief. And God must be grieved.

There is only one way we can change this: humble ourselves, pray, and seek God. We must confess our sin and change our ways. Let's commit to pray for our beloved nation—the land of our birth and of our choice.

Making It Personal

How can I pray for my country today?

One Woman

Deborah, the wife of Lappidoth, was a prophet who had become a judge
in Israel....The Israelites came to her to settle their disputes.
Judges 4:4-5

One of my favorite Bible characters is Deborah. She was a leader during a very dark period in ancient Israel's history. What a strong leader and encourager she was.

At this time, the nation faced a very intimidating enemy army. They really didn't have much of a chance. While Deborah had trust in God and a positive outlook, poor Barak the warrior did not. Barak had heard God's command to lead, but he chose to listen to his fears. "The enemy is so huge, and we're supposed to sit and wait for them? Okay, I'll go, but only if you go with me, Deborah!" He sounded a bit whiney in this story. But Deborah showed leadership. She told Barak she would go, and that the Lord's victory would be at the hands of a woman!

So off they went, this one woman marching alongside Barak and 10,000 soldiers. Deborah was proactive in a culture that was very dangerous, negative, and threatening.

What do you do when things happen that are out of your control? Do you whine? Or, like Deborah, do you lead positively? In this unstable, negative world in which we live, may we all have a positive, uplifting influence.

Making It Personal

What do I see in Deborah that I would like to emulate?

July 6

Love Never Fails

Without love I would be no good to anybody.
1 Corinthians 13:2

Two mountain goats approached one another on a narrow ledge. Realizing there was no room to pass, over and over again they reared and bucked, locking horns to see which could overpower the other, but neither budged. Finally the more sensible one knelt down and let the other climb over him, and they both went merrily on their way.

That's a beautiful illustration of being long-suffering—an aspect of love. Sometimes we must let people walk over us (which is not the same as walking *on* us) if we are going to help them. Love takes the time to share and care.

Our love can be demonstrated in so many ways. Love always supports and protects. Love believes the best and takes the kindest view of people—it searches for the good. Love is permanent. Love never fails; it is always in style.

Love is:

- slow to suspect, quick to trust;
- slow to offend, quick to defend;
- slow to hinder, quick to help;
- slow to demand, quick to give.

Love is a big part of success.

Making It Personal

How can I show love to someone on the job today?

Servant Leader

Since I, the Lord and Teacher, have washed your feet,
you ought to wash each other's feet.
John 13:14

Serving others, giving all you have to them, can be exhausting. And at the same time, it is so worthwhile. The most effective leaders are servants.

Jesus is our greatest example of a servant leader, especially when He washed the disciples' feet. Jesus served His disciples because He loved them (John 13:1). However, the main reason He washed the disciples' feet was as an example. He wanted to show the disciples that they were to be full-time servers of men and women.

Why is it so hard to become a servant leader? That's easy. We all want to be numero uno—*there is no one better than me!* That is a struggle. Power is an important issue for a leader.

So how do we overcome our power hunger? Just like Jesus did. He didn't forget His authority (see John 13:3), but he looked upon His disciples as His brothers. We, likewise, will serve those we lead if we choose to view them as our brothers and sisters.

Making It Personal

What is one act of selfless service I can perform today?

Seven Points of Leadership

*You have been faithful in handling this small amount,
so now I will give you many more responsibilities.*
Matthew 25:23

It's important for leaders to know what they are responsible for. If you are a leader in some capacity at work, remember that you represent your company. You are modeling for others how to do business and how to become leaders themselves. Here are seven helpful points for all leaders to remember:

1. We are responsible for our own actions.
2. We are responsible for the care of those we are leading.
3. We are responsible to develop the gifts God has given us.
4. We are responsible to know what we believe and why we believe it.
5. We are responsible to be a servant.
6. We are responsible to do what is right.
7. We are responsible to encourage one another.

Who are leaders ultimately responsible to? God, our heavenly Father. So lead well.

Making It Personal

Which one of these seven points do I need to work on the most?

Guard Your Heart

Above all else, guard your heart, for it affects everything you do.
Proverbs 4:23

The book of Proverbs is a compilation of advice from a father to his son. Here the father warns, "Guard your heart."

When we read in the Bible about the *heart*, it is not speaking about the organ in our chest that pumps blood. Rather, it is describing our whole inner being. In other words, guard your mind, guard your emotions, guard your will—your whole inner being.

Why is this so important? Because your heart affects everything you do. How you respond, what you say, how you act, these things all flow out of your mind, inner emotions, and will. So be a guarded person—in the good sense!

Making It Personal

What does it mean to me to guard my emotions?

A Huge Small Problem

The tongue is a small thing, but what enormous damage it can do.
A tiny spark can set a great forest on fire.
James 3:5

One of the parts of our body that gets a great deal of exercise and very little rest is the tongue. The way we exercise this little muscle surely means that our tongue should be in good shape! But is it really?

We don't examine our tongues very often. We don't buy cosmetics for it, nor do we make weekly appointments at the tongue beautician. Yet, it is our tongues, not our clothes, attractive haircut, or wealth that determines our true inner beauty. Our reputation will be established by how we use our tongues because of its lasting impression on people.

According to an encyclopedia article, about three million acres of trees are destroyed by fire in our country every year. About half of these trees are destroyed by lightning; the other half by human beings. A very small fire, even from a spark, quickly spreads. It is the same with fires set by the tongue. James warns us about the lasting damage this tiny body part can do.

Make sure you exercise your tongue in the right way by keeping it free of gossip, truthful, contented, kind, and helpful.

Making It Personal

What kind of exercise is my tongue getting?

Humble Dedication

The humble will see their God at work and be glad.
Let all who seek God's help live in joy.
Psalm 69:32

It is rare to find a person who is fully dedicated and truly humble.

Dedication is having a passionate belief in something. There's no stopping a leader when they are dedicated. Passionate commitment is the basis for great works of art, inventions, as well as scientific discoveries and explorations. It is what makes marriages, corporations, and governments work. Dedicated workers do better work, and they do it joyfully. In our particular business, being dedicated means we believe in our company's Philosophy, Purpose, and Plan.

Humility is something that actually comes out of having a healthy view of yourself—ever think about it that way? If you know who you are and have a healthy ego (which is okay), you can accept compliments graciously and take intelligent criticism without pouting and reacting. You can be generous in forgiving others because you realize how much you need forgiveness yourself. (If you see someone who never forgives or never takes responsibility for wrong actions, they are not humble, but self-important.)

Strive to be a person of humble dedication to whatever task you face today.

Making It Personal

What are the things I am dedicated to right now?

Follow the Plow

I am focusing all my energies on this one thing:
Forgetting the past and looking forward to what lies ahead.
Philippians 3:13

Pastor A.W. Tozer observed that miracles don't just happen—they follow the plow. In other words, a bountiful harvest comes from a lot of hard work. After seeking God's guidance in a matter, we must do our share by "pushing the plow."

We must also be forward-thinking. Jesus said, "Anyone who puts a hand to the plow and then looks back is not fit for the Kingdom of God" (Luke 9:62). Reviewing where we have been has its benefits, but in order to succeed, we must forget past mistakes and focus on what we can do in the future, "looking forward to what lies ahead."

The farmer behind his plow doesn't see the harvest as he plows, but he knows it will come eventually. Our faithful plowing may not yield immediate results, but we'll see them in time. No matter what our job, if we are diligent, we can expect to have a harvest—in God's time.

Success is found in looking ahead and working hard. Miracles follow the plow!

Making It Personal

How can I be more forward-looking?

Choosing Thankfulness

We thank you, O God! We give thanks because you are near.
Psalm 75:1

I once read a story about an elderly woman who was bed-ridden. Her hands were tightly contracted, and her whole body was crippled with rheumatism. For sixteen years she had not moved from her bed, or looked out of the window, or even lifted her hand to her own face. She was in constant pain.

But she had a two-pronged fork fastened to a stick, which she could hold with her thumb. She used this to put on her spectacles and to feed herself. And there was another thing she did with her fork: she turned the pages of a large Bible within her reach.

A visitor remarked that she was all alone. "Yes," she said cheerfully, "I am alone; but yet not alone. The Lord is constantly with me. I have laid here for sixteen years, yet I have much to praise the Lord for. I have a thumb that works!"

What a remarkable woman—a woman with a thankful heart. Could we pass that test? Can we bring joy to our heavenly Father by always being thankful, no matter what?

Making It Personal

**What is one thing I can be thankful for, even
if my circumstances are difficult?**

July 14

Make Someone's Day

*Work with enthusiasm, as though you were
working for the LORD rather than for people.*
Ephesians 6:7

People crave personal attention. We can buy just about anything you could ever need or want in malls, boutiques, kiosks, or even online. But we cannot buy personal caring.

Once, I was staying at a very fine hotel in California. I picked up the phone to call room service and a voice said, "I'm putting you on hold." Well, that's the same as telling me, "I'm putting you on *ignore*." I would have preferred a more personal touch. (Actually, the hotel's overall service was wonderful. That one incident just made a good illustration of my point!) People are hungry for one-on-one contact and personal consideration of their individual needs. It's not always convenient or easy to do, but it is so needed. By taking time to assist others or just listen to them, you are actually serving God.

Go ahead—make someone's day, and by doing so, you will please the Lord!

Making It Personal

How can I delight God by personally serving someone today?

When You've Had Enough

*[Elijah] sat down under a solitary broom tree and prayed
that he might die. "I have had enough, LORD," he said.*
1 Kings 19:4

The prophet Elijah was tired and discouraged. After one of his greatest successes (the victory over the priests of Baal at Mt. Carmel), he had outrun a chariot all the way to Jezreel. Then Queen Jezebel threatened to kill him. So Elijah fled, withdrawing alone to the desert.

God's response to Elijah's depression was pointed and practical, and it can help us when we are down. First, God told Elijah, "Get up and eat!" (1 Kings 19:5). In other words, the prophet was to take care of his body. The lesson for us: When we are tired, rest. When we are weary, eat well. We don't need to let busyness or discouragement keep us from getting sleep and eating nourishing food.

Second, the Lord said to Elijah, "Go out and stand before me on the mountain" (verse 11). Then God sent a windstorm, an earthquake, and a fire, but God was not in those big blustery things. God was heard in a still, small voice. Elijah had to get quiet and get his eyes off himself and onto God. The lesson for us: Remember that we are never alone in our difficulties. We need to take time to be quiet so we can hear God's still, small voice.

Making It Personal

How can I respond more wisely to setbacks and discouragement?

July 16

The Fruit of Learning

*I, the LORD, search all hearts and examine secret motives. I give
all people their due rewards, according to what their actions deserve.*
Jeremiah 17:10

I have been involved in the corporate world for more than thirty years, and I am still learning. As my husband says, our training goes on forever. Here are some things I have learned about being in business:

1. The quality of service is important if we want to build a lasting business. Service makes the difference! It is our survival kit.
2. Integrity in business dealings must be beyond reproach. This means we must build relationships of trust with both customers and colleagues.
3. Our actions and way of doing business build our own reputation as well as that of our company. We need to represent both well.
4. Our number one purpose should be to honor God and to serve people. Keep in mind that all people need love and attention.

God has given you this day to use as you will. You can waste it or you can use it for good. What you do with these hours is important, because you are exchanging a day of your life for it.

Making It Personal

*Which of the four items above do I need to
incorporate more into my business?*

Don't Blow It

*A wise woman builds her house; a foolish woman
tears hers down with her own hands.*
Proverbs 14:1

A nn Landers once said, "Someday the liberated woman will discover that her most important job, the one with the greatest rewards, was right under her nose—and she blew it." She was talking about motherhood, of course.

Are you a mother, or hoping to be a mother someday? Don't let your work, as important as that is, keep you from training your children and being with them at critical stages of their experience.

When our boys were in high school, they played football. The season started in August when the coach began two-a-day practices. For three weeks, morning and afternoon, the coach had the team running, blocking, and throwing over and over again. My boys would come home exhausted, only to get up hours later and do it all again. The real test of their training came during the opening game in September, which proved whether the fundamentals had been learned.

As mothers, we, too, are to "train a child in the way he should go" (Proverbs 22:6 NIV). We can have success in business and many other areas, but if we fail to train our children in the fundamentals of life, we have really blown it.

Making It Personal

What do I need to do to make my children a priority in my life?

𝒫 𝒮 & 𝒞

*Whenever we have the opportunity, we should do good to everyone,
especially to our Christian brothers and sisters.*
Galatians 6:10

Most corporations focus on S & P—*sales and profit.*
Our company focuses on P & S—*people and service.*
There is a big difference. People are the most important
asset to our company. And service is a way of life. From
my experience, I have to say that P & S is the key to real
success in business.

But there is one more thing I want to add to the P & S
mix: *caring.* If your colleagues and customers know that
you really care about them, you will have little problem
winning their gratitude and loyalty.

Be a P S & C (*people, service,* and *caring*) businesswoman. If you remember this acronym, it will go a long
way toward making you successful in the years ahead.
This world is quickly moving away from God's principles
and values. Having a P S & C focus is the biblical way to
live and do business.

Making It Personal

How can I offer greater service and caring to people?

Payday Someday

*People can get many good things by the words they say; the work
of their hands also gives them many benefits.*
Proverbs 12:14

The book of Proverbs tells us that we are often rewarded by the things we say and do. We read something similar in Galatians 6:7: "Don't be misled. . . . You will always reap what you sow!" In other words, payday will come someday.

When our children were little, they knew about "payday." If they didn't behave, they would reap the consequences! But there is also a good kind of payday— a recompense for treating others right. If we have sown kindness, we will reap kindness.

Simple acts of goodness are rewarded in time. What about being a friend to a colleague whose mother passed away? Or offering a smile at the door as you welcome guests? Or sharing food with those in need? That caring spirit will come back to you someday.

Why do we do good things for others? Not for any reward. Not for any thanks. Not for any return. However, it's just the law of reaping and sowing that God has set up. A giving spirit will be returned again and again. Take time to sow good things into people's lives.

Making It Personal

Into whose life will I plant seeds of kindness today?

From Little to Much

Commit your work to the LORD, and then your plans will succeed.
Proverbs 16:3

The first recorded baseball game in history was played in Beachville, Ontario, Canada, just five miles from my birth city of Woodstock. I have loved baseball since I was a small girl, even though I never had any encouragement to follow the game. I have never really understood, in fact, why I love baseball so much. Maybe the reason is simply that I was born so close to Beachville, that nostalgic place in history.

Baseball is a game, but it is also hard work that takes diligence and commitment. The same is true for our jobs. What we do for a living can be exciting and interesting, but it is *work*.

Committing our work to the Lord means expecting great things to happen and then working to bring them about. After all, little is much when God is in it. Hard work might seem to take the gusto out of us, but with God in charge, we are on our way to the World Series!

Isn't it time for you to commit—or to recommit—your work to the Lord?

Making It Personal

How can I work diligently without burning out?

July 21

Doing Something New

*I am about to do a brand-new thing. See, I have
already begun! Do you not see it?*
Isaiah 43:19

One morning a professor was dressing and began
to button his vest. His fingers were going along as
usual in their intricate operations when a button wouldn't
button. By mistake his daughter had sewn up one of
the buttonholes. The professor's fingers fumbled for a
moment, and then he realized something. His fingers
could "remember" what to do without his mind even
thinking about it; it is called physiological memory.

After this discovery, the professor found that as long
as his students kept on doing the things they had always
done, their minds wouldn't really work. It was only when
he figuratively sewed up their buttonholes—hid their
notebooks, changed their routine, threatened them with
failure—that they did any creative thinking. He came
to the startling conclusion that it is only when the old
order of things won't work any longer that the mind gets
creative on the job.

Want to be open to new ideas? Break out of your
routine. And then, when you discover a fresh idea, share it
with a friend or associate.

Making It Personal

How can I jolt myself out of my ruts?

Chasing a Dead Dog

*Who is the king of Israel trying to catch anyway? Should he spend
his time chasing one who is as worthless as a dead dog?*
1 Samuel 24:14

A woman was taking care of her neighbor's dog while the
neighbor was away. Suddenly the old dog died. The
humane society agreed to arrange a burial if the woman
would bring in the remains. Since the woman had to go
there by bus, she decided to put the dog in an old suitcase
and carry him to his final resting place.

While she was changing buses, a fellow offered to
carry her piece of luggage. She looked back just in time to
see the culprit absconding down an alley with the suitcase.
Her first impulse was to give chase, but then she was struck
by the absurdity of the situation. "Chasing a dead dog—of
all things!"

This is a dramatic illustration for us, both in our
personal lives and with our business relationships. Have
we ever chased a dead dog? Do we ever run down an old
alley, trying to recapture the past? As difficult as it is to
accept, all of the past is history. Any efforts toward reliving
periods of our lives are futile attempts to regain what is
gone forever. We are to learn from the past, apply it to the
present, and dream for the future.

Making It Personal

What "dead dog" have I been chasing lately?

Moving Dirt

*A gossip goes around revealing secrets, but those
who are trustworthy can keep a confidence.*
Proverbs 11:13

Outstanding Christian businessman R. G. LeTourneau headed up a company that manufactured large earth-moving equipment in Longview, Texas. LeTourneau had many wonderful stories to tell, including a story about one of the machines his company used to make. It was called the "Model G."

One day someone asked LeTourneau, "What does the 'G' stand for?" He thought it was probably the middle initial of LeTourneau's name.

LeTourneau replied to the man, "The 'G' stands for gossip, because like a talebearer, this machine moves a lot of dirt—and moves it fast!"

Have you been "moving dirt" by gossiping? It's easy to do, and one can easily pick up the bad habit from others. But gossip destroys trust and damages relationships. It can even ruin a career. Don't participate in gossip.

Making It Personal

Am I a gossip? If so, what will I do to change?

Model of Integrity

Let everything you do reflect the integrity and seriousness of your teaching.
Titus 2:7

In the first state golf tournament Tom Watson ever entered, he put his putter down behind the ball on one of the greens. To his surprise, the ball moved slightly. No one saw it—he was certain of that—but he knew the ball had moved.

Placing his personal integrity ahead of his desire to win, Tom went to an official and told him, "My ball moved." His admission cost him a stroke and he lost the hole. Happily, as it turned out, he did win the match. But more importantly, he was able to live with an unblemished conscience.

Tom Watson modeled his convictions, and that's what we must do in our businesses. You may say, "Well, let my company have whatever standards it wants. I can do as I please."

Is that true? No, I don't think so. You see, you represent your company, and in fact, you may be the only part of your company that your neighbor ever sees. Your personal integrity is on the line, but so is the integrity of the company. That's why you must model honesty and fairness at all times.

Making It Personal

How can I model integrity in my business dealings?

With God's Help

All the people rejoiced greatly because of what God had done for the people, for everything had been accomplished so quickly.
2 Chronicles 29:36 (*Verse of the Year 1996*)

When Hezekiah came to the throne in Jerusalem, his first priority was to reopen the doors of the Temple. King Hezekiah had a set purpose: to make the Temple worthy of the service to be performed there.

The priests cleaned it up and prepared for worship. When the goal was realized, the king and all the people rejoiced that God had helped them accomplish it so quickly.

Isn't that the way it is with us? As we look back at our careers, we marvel at how quickly the time has passed and are amazed at all that God has done for us in that time. It is God who helps us succeed. Like the priests, we work and prepare, but it is God who undergirds it all. Let us be grateful to Him for His abundant blessings.

Making It Personal

What has God accomplished for me in my career?

The Glory of Nature

The heavens are yours, and the earth is yours;
everything in the world is yours—you created it all.
Psalm 89:11

Isn't God's creation amazing? Take the great horned owl, for example. They build their nests during the late winter months, rather than in the warmer spring months as other birds. They do this because small prey for food is much easier to find without foliage in which to hide.

Now, baby owls grow from three inches to two feet in only three months! They need a great deal of food very quickly. In winter, the parents have the advantage of catching these needed meals more easily. What amazing instincts God gave to Father and Mother owl!

That is just one animal among thousands of species. What details of beauty and awe are found in every part of God's wonderful creation! He is awesome.

Making It Personal

Take some time to take a walk, watch some birds, or just
look around and notice the glory of God's creation.

One Happy Family

All of you should be of one mind, full of sympathy toward each other, loving one another with tender hearts and humble minds. Don't repay evil for evil. Don't retaliate when people say unkind things about you. Instead, pay them back with a blessing. That is what God wants you to do, and he will bless you for it.
1 Peter 3:8-9

The phrase "one big happy family" conjures up images of well-behaved children and perfect parents all smiling as they gather around the dinner table. I don't know about your family, but our family wasn't always that idyllic. Yet, the Bible encourages us to "live in harmony with one another" (1 Peter 3:8 NIV), and the verses above give some hints for how to do that.

"Be full of sympathy." Sympathy is feeling another's hurt or burden, participating in their joys and sorrows.

"Love one another with tender hearts." We must have gentle love without judging.

"Don't repay evil with evil…pay them back with a blessing." Go further than just refraining from an evil payback; bless that person with an unexpected kindness.

Participating in a happy family system—at home or at work—means giving smiles, not sneers; compliments, not complaints; cooperation, not competition.

Making It Personal

What is one way I can live more in harmony with my family? With my coworkers?

The Treasure of Friendship

As iron sharpens iron, a friend sharpens a friend.
Proverbs 27:17

We need friends. They multiply our joys and divide our sorrows. They serve as mirrors to show us things about ourselves we need to see. Friendships are stronger many times than family relationships. We are able to relax and allow more easily for the faults of our friends.

I had a call the other night from a friend. Andy asked, "Who was that? What did she want?" I answered, "Nothing. We just wanted to talk together." Women enjoy talking and visiting and just being together. Men like to get together, but more often than not they will *do* something—watch TV, play soccer, go to ball games, go fishing. Many men don't seem to feel the need for deeper friendships.

It's easy to understand our need for deeper friendships. Some studies have shown that women who have close friends are happier in their marriages. That is the "keeping it personal" side of each of us. Without friends my life would not be complete. I have no doubt that most of you agree with me. Our friends become real treasures.

Making It Personal

When has a good friend helped multiply my joy or divide my sorrow?

Time Well Spent

See then that you walk circumspectly, not as fools but as wise,
redeeming the time, because the days are evil.
Ephesians 5:15-16 (NKJV)

What does it mean to redeem something? If we redeem a coupon, we are trading it in for something of more value. When we redeem frequent flier miles, we're getting it back on a future flight. If a baseball player redeems himself, he gets an RBI base hit to make up for an error in the previous inning. To *redeem* literally means "to buy back."

We all have twenty-four hours in a day, and the Bible reminds us to be wise and "redeem" that time, to buy it back by making the most of it. To do that, it helps to define the priorities for our lives. I believe that we need to have our relationship with God first, then our family, and then our work.

Interruptions are unavoidable, and sometimes they make us revise our time budget. However, we can still "redeem the time," since an interruption is often God's way of giving us unexpected opportunities to help others. And that's always time well spent.

Making It Personal

Am I spending my time wisely?

July 30

What's Your Color?

*You are the light of the world—like a city on a mountain,
glowing in the night for all to see.*
Matthew 5:14

Light contains all the colors. Just look at the range of colors reflected in a drop of water when the sunlight hits it.

Did you know that some people think our color preference reveals the kind of person we are? For fun, let's explore the colors and what qualities they supposedly stand for.

Red: ambitious, extroverted, adventurous, impulsive, willing to follow uncharted paths

Orange: creative, intuitive, artistic, outgoing, competent, organized, cheerful

Yellow: idealistic, perfectionistic, having a flair with words, persistent, people-oriented

Green: reliable, compassionate, tolerant of others' shortcomings, strong communication abilities, service-oriented, benevolent

Blue: sweet, deep thinking, self-reliant, responsible, intelligent, demanding

Purple: creative, perceptive, encouraging

Let your own light shine, whatever color and qualities you represent!

Making It Personal
Which of these color qualities do I have?

Planning to Succeed

*Wise people think before they act;
fools don't and even brag about it!*
Proverbs 13:16

A plan is an organized list of the actions. Planning is the first step toward reaching a goal.

The Bible mentions many events in which planning was key. Noah planned the building of the ark. Moses planned the building of the tabernacle. Solomon planned the building of the Temple. God always honored those who planned.

The quality of the planning determines the quality of performance. Boxing champions, for example, don't become champions in the ring; their supremacy is merely recognized in the ring. Becoming a champion happens in their *daily routine*. Likewise, star employees don't become stars just when they are recognized at an awards banquet, but they become proven employees as they plan and work every day, every week, every month.

So, remember the old adage: If you fail to plan, you plan to fail.

Making It Personal

What should I be planning now so that I can accomplish it later?

August

Jesus taught the principle that the greater the service, the greater the leader. Be a leader who serves.

With love,
Joan

The Lesson of the Shoreline

I, the LORD, am the one who defines the ocean's sandy shoreline,
an everlasting boundary that the waters cannot cross.
Jeremiah 5:22

When we can, Andy and I enjoy the opportunity to relax on the Gulf of Mexico in Florida. Summer there means moonlight over the ocean, windsurfers, boats bringing in shrimp, porpoises jumping out of the water (I wish I could listen in on their conversations), and lots of children playing in the surf. Summer is my favorite time of the year!

As I look out at that mighty ocean and realize how long it has been rolling, roaring, and never ceasing, I think of a verse Jeremiah wrote. "Do you have no respect for me?" God said. "Why do you not tremble in my presence? I, the LORD, am the one who defines the ocean's sandy shoreline, an everlasting boundary that the waters cannot cross. The waves may toss and roar, but they can never pass the bounds I set" (Jeremiah 5:22). Isn't such a God to be feared and worshiped?

Being at the beach is always special to us because of the constant reminders of a marvelous God—the One who sets the bounds of the sea, the One who has blessed us so very much, the One who loves us with an everlasting love.

Making It Personal

What element of nature helps me feel closer to God?

The Personal Touch

Jesus took him by the hand and helped him to his feet, and he stood up.
Mark 9:27

Imagine that we are playing *Jeopardy* and I give you this definition: "Having to do with the character and personality of a certain person."

You say, "What is the meaning of 'personal'?"

You win!

Keeping it personal—dealing with real people in real ways—is a passion of mine. As businesses grow, it becomes harder and harder to maintain the personal touch. Technology tends to take over. I often wonder how we used to do bookkeeping with just an adding machine, paper, and pencil! How did we keep inventory straight? So technology is a wonderful creation for complex businesses. But we mustn't let it take the place of the personal element.

No matter what the challenges are, we must keep our businesses personal. Jesus found ways to serve all kinds of different people in very personal ways. You can find ways to keep your business personal, too, through sending personal letters and making personal phone calls. Make it your goal to be known for your personal touch.

Making It Personal

How can I put the personal touch back into my business dealings?

Repeat, Repeat, Repeat

Spend your time and energy in training yourself for spiritual fitness.
1 Timothy 4:7

Any good training, means repetition, repetition, and more repetition. Why do you suppose coaches make their players repeat drills? They want those players to go over the basics so often that when they are in a competitive mode, the plays are a part of them. Their reaction comes naturally. They see the "opposition" so much during training that when they see the actual defenses during the game, they are able to use the correct plays.

Now, how does this apply to the workplace?

First: We must recognize that training is
         important even though it isn't always easy.
Second: Repeat, repeat, repeat!
Third: Do it!

When we are committed to a job, we will be willing to practice over and over so that our words and actions become second nature to us and we can focus on the people we are serving.

Making It Personal

**What are some new things I want to learn
—or practice again—this week?**

August 4

Genuine Caring

I have no one else like Timothy, who genuinely cares about your welfare.
Philippians 2:20

The apostle Paul told the Christians at Philippi that his young protégé Timothy "genuinely cares about your welfare." Following in Timothy's footsteps, you must decide that you will be genuinely interested in the welfare of others and that you won't expect to be served. That's not easy, is it?

If you are going to be a servant leader, you need to know whom you will serve. These should be the people you manage and those who are lower than you in the company structure. If you understand that, then you will have accountability to others. So remember whom you are serving.

Paul was honest when he said, "I have no one else like Timothy, who genuinely cares about your welfare. All the others care only for themselves and not for what matters to Jesus Christ" (Philippians 2:20-21). That is a sad statement. Yet true servant leaders are hard to find.

Jesus taught the principle that *the greater the service, the greater the leader.* Do you want to be great? Then be a leader who serves your people.

Making It Personal

Who should I be caring for, and how?

Believing, Hoping, Loving

I want to share my joy with all of you.
Philippians 2:17

Joy is not how your face looks—it is the status of your heart. Happiness can make you smile, but it passes away. Happiness on this particular day—August 5—reminds me of celebrating Andy's birthday in a unique way one year. I gave him his number two son, Tommy, for his birthday gift. We are still smiling with joy!

Joy abides as gladness of the heart, an inner feeling. How do we get joy? Consider this quote from John Lancaster Spalding: "It is by believing, hoping, loving, and doing for others that one finds joy." I think that is such a great statement. Believing, hoping, loving, doing for others = JOY!

Real joy comes from believing in the Lord Jesus Christ and then hoping, loving, and doing for others. In the workplace, joy comes through positive and focused people who are excited about what they are doing. If people know that they are truly making a positive difference in others' lives, they will radiate joy!

Making It Personal

Do I reflect the joy of doing for others?

August 6

The Whole Truth

Fix your thoughts on what is true and honorable and right.
Philippians 4:8

I resolve, just for today, to avoid exaggeration, white lies, misleading statements, innuendo, unverified rumors, or anything that might deceive." Unfortunately, many of us would be unable to handle this assignment for one day. When it comes to truthfulness, our tongues can be pretty careless in the following ways.

1. *Boasting.* The ancient word used for *braggart* in the Bible means literally "a wandering quack." A braggart usually boasts about things that he can't control, including himself. Let other people praise you.

2. *Exaggeration.* This is nothing more than decorating the truth to fit our own agenda.

3. *Lying.* Mark Twain said, "When in doubt, tell the truth. It will confound your enemies and astound your friends." It's always best to tell the truth.

4. *Gossip.* Even if something is true, we don't need to spread it around.

Fixing your thoughts on what is good and true can fix the problem of the tongue.

Making It Personal

Can I "tell the whole truth and nothing but the truth" for an entire day?

A Lovely Choice

*If I gave everything I have to the poor and . . . didn't love others,
I would be of no value whatsoever.*
1 Corinthians 13:3

What a difference it would make if we could simply love others! Love is a choice we make. It is not based on how we feel or on someone else's behavior, but on the fact that God has told us to do it. If we don't have love, all the other things we do are worthless.

Love is not choosy; it is inclusive. Jesus said, "Love your enemies" (Matthew 5:44).

Love seeks another person's highest good. Condoning sin or approving of wrong actions is not love. We are to "correct . . . when necessary" (Titus 2:15).

Love tells the truth. Flattering someone just to make them feel good or to get something from them is not honest. The apostle Paul said, "Speak the truth in love" (Ephesians 4:15 NIV). The Greek word used there literally means "truthing it in love." I hope we are all truthing it in love—not fudging the truth.

Love is active. "Let us stop just saying we love each other; let us really show it by our actions" (1 John 3:18). We may never achieve perfect love, but we can take the first step today.

Making It Personal

Am I choosing to actively demonstrate my love for others?

Golden Friendship

The heartfelt counsel of a friend is as sweet as perfume and incense.
Proverbs 27:9

Through the years God has gifted me with wonderful friends. I have sweet friends by the hundreds across this nation and in many other countries as well.

New friends are special, and it is always exciting for me to make new relationships. However, our long-lasting friendships stick together like glue.

When business circumstances or relocations occur to separate friends, it is one of the most difficult things to live with. True friendships, though, last through those challenges. I am blessed with so many "old" friends who remain involved in my life. As the old rhyme says:

> *Make new friends,*
> *But keep the old.*
> *One is silver,*
> *And the other gold.*

I have silver and I have gold! What a priceless treasure.

Making It Personal

Who are the "silver" and "gold" friends in my life?

What Are You Building?

The entire building was completed in every detail by midautumn of the eleventh year of [Solomon's] reign. So it took seven years to build the Temple.
1 Kings 6:38

When King Solomon built the glorious new Temple in Jerusalem, it took him seven years to complete. In our day of instant everything, that's hard to fathom. Solomon used nothing but the best materials and the best craftsmen for the Lord's Temple. He took the time it needed and he didn't rush the process. The result? A magnificent one-of-a-kind Temple for worshiping Almighty God.

I know you are not building a temple any time soon, but let's think for a moment about what you are building. In your personal relationships, you are building something strong with the stones of positive words and encouragement. In your spiritual life, you are building a solid foundation with the stones of prayer and worship. In your work, you are building a strong business with the stones of integrity and creativity.

Don't worry too much about how long it may take to get the results you want. Like Solomon, just focus on building all these areas of your life with the very best you can give.

Making It Personal

What kind of life do I want to build?

Principles Not Performance

Solomon also built a palace for himself, and it took him thirteen years to complete the construction. . . . He had seven hundred wives and three hundred concubines. And sure enough, they led his heart away from the LORD.
1 Kings 7:1; 11:3-4

Solomon blew it. He was faithful to God at first, and he worked seven years to build the Temple. But then we read that he went on to build a palace for himself that was even grander and that took almost twice as long to build! I think Solomon had his priorities a bit messed up. He was concerned about his own pleasure and image and performance, forgetting to be a principled person who obeyed God. Doing things his way eventually got him into real trouble and ruined the legacy he left to his splintered nation.

The company Andy and I started is built on some basic principles. Our purpose is to honor God and serve people. We seek to operate with integrity and honesty. We have never been performance-driven, but are people-driven.

Make it your goal to be first and foremost a person of principles, not just performance. This will result in leaving a rich legacy to those who come after you.

Making It Personal

What are some of the principles I want to live by?

Be a Role Model

*Keep putting into practice all you learned from me
and heard from me and saw me doing.*
Philippians 4:9

A re you a leader in your business? If so, I have a request for you. *Please* keep your word. Tell the truth. Keep your promises. Let your word be as good as gold, and let your actions prove it. Then others will know they can depend on you.

If you don't think others are paying attention to what you say and do, think again. People watch us! The apostle Paul urged the Philippians to copy his positive example. Could you say to those you lead, "Keep putting into practice all you have learned from me and have seen me doing"? Are you modeling what it means to be a hard worker? Do you have integrity and honesty? Keep practicing these things so that others will do likewise.

Making It Personal

*Who have been my role models? Would I want
someone else to copy my life?*

August 12

Running in Circles

Those who wait on the LORD will find new strength.
They . . . will run and not grow weary.
Isaiah 40:31

Most of us have a tendency to run in circles—both in our personal life and in our business. In Isaiah 40:31, God is saying, "Slow down. Trust Me completely, and if you do that, I will lead you when you are running. I will direct your path, and then when you run, you will not grow weary." God said He is the everlasting God and He never grows weary or faint. He has the power to direct our running. No more circles.

In our business we can enrich other people's lives as we run. What a joy that is! As God directs our running, we become more focused and fruitful, not tired and frustrated.

And what has God promised for those who trust completely in Him? They will find new strength. What a great promise to remember on days we need help to stop running in circles.

Making It Personal

What causes me to run in circles and
forget God's power to direct me?

The Art of Integrity

The LORD demands fairness in every business deal; he sets the standard.
Proverbs 16:11
(Founding Verse of Premier Designs, November 1985)

I read about a woman named Chin-Ning Chu who gave lectures on "The Art of Deceit" that is practiced regularly in Chinese businesses. You say, "Well, we're not like that here in America." Don't be too sure.

What about well-publicized stockbrokers' deceptions? What about the lies we hear from television preachers? Our government is not immune either, with politicians accused of a lack of integrity. If we're honest, we can see that even here in our beloved country the art of deceit is practiced. And what about our personal lives? Are we truthful with our tax forms, even when we are alone? Do we practice integrity at home as well as in the public eye?

Vernon Grounds defines *integrity* as "the antithesis of hypocrisy, sound all the way through, like a gold coin without alloy." The Hebrew root word for integrity indicates something solid, of substance. A person of *integrity* is complete, whole, solid. Let's put our lives under the spotlight of God's Word and let His loving truth transform us into people of integrity.

Making It Personal

*In what ways can I fight deceit in
my life and practice integrity?*

Pure Motives

*People may think they are doing what is right,
but the LORD examines the heart.*
Proverbs 21:2

Why do you do what you do? We all have very different motives for having a job. What are yours?

The Bible teaches that God is as interested in our motives as He is in our behavior. We all know how easy it is to do the right thing for very wrong reasons. We can give to others just to get something from them. We can serve with a smile, while underneath we're just angry. We can pretend to work a business because we believe in it, but all the time we are greedy and there just to make money.

Proverbs 21:2 shows that people may think they are doing right, but the Lord examines the heart. God sees everything. We can't fool Him. So let's make sure our motives are pure as we work our business. If they are, then we can honestly promote our company's Philosophy and Purpose.

Do you honestly believe that your business is a good one? Then share the opportunity with a clear conscience. Do you truly feel that your product or service is of high quality? Then share that with your customers. God loves a pure heart and will bless you as you act out of right motives.

Making It Personal

What are my motives for doing what I do?

You Are . . .

Every day of my life was recorded in your book. Every moment was laid out before a single day had passed.
Psalm 139:16

When the first seven astronauts were chosen for the space program, they were selected in part by the way they finished the simple statement "I am . . . " ("I am a pilot from Florida," etc.). I'm going to turn that around into "You are . . ."

- ☞ You are special.
- ☞ You are needed.
- ☞ You are important.
- ☞ You are wonderful.

God knows who you are. Read Psalm 139:13-17 and see how He formed you and has known you from the very start. He knows every part of your life—even the parts that haven't happened yet! Isn't that awesome?

God is sovereign, and the work He has begun in us He will finish. Why? Because He planned it all before we were ever born. Doesn't that excite you? It excites me.

However, just because God has planned every day of our lives, that does not give us license to sit around and let God do it all. We must be willing to work and to fit into God's plan and purpose.

Making It Personal

How would I finish the sentence, "I am . . . "? How does this compare with who God says I am?

How to Succeed

*Commit your work to the LORD,
and then your plans will succeed.*
Proverbs 16:3

Success comes before work only in the dictionary. Throughout the Bible we are encouraged to be people of diligence, committed to the tasks in life that need to be accomplished.

Some think this is a drag rather than a privilege. For those people laziness is a reality. They find it difficult to get started. They are defensive and negative. They are quitters and live by excuses.

Diligence and hard work are both needed to be successful. Your work—of any kind—will be of little value if you don't try hard. Constant effort is needed to accomplish goals you have set.

Now, this does not mean you need to shift your priorities in your business relationships. You should still be putting God first in your life, family second, and career third. But I am encouraging you, even as Proverbs encourages all of us, to commit your work to the Lord. Commit your meetings to the Lord. Commit your colleagues to the Lord. And commit your service to your customers to the Lord. That is the way to have success.

Making It Personal

How can I work harder and commit my work to God?

Busy as Ants

Take a lesson from the ants, you lazybones.
Learn from their ways and be wise!
Proverbs 6:6

My experience with ants is not unlike yours, I'm sure. You can't get rid of them. Ants never, never give up. Ever see a lazy ant? They all are busy—each one producing, each one highly motivated.

Ants get the essentials done first, such as gathering food. They work without a foreman. They work ahead of time so that they can relax later. And they do it all without anyone else rewarding them.

God says that if we want to be wise, we have only to look at the ants. Work is not a curse to them. Work is a privilege, a challenge for ants. And it should be the same for us. Work helps us to serve others. It is an answer to boredom, a place to invest our energy. It is God's plan to provide for our physical needs.

The ant is a tiny insect that can be stepped on and have its life snuffed out at any given moment, yet it keeps on keeping on. So why don't we?

Making It Personal

In what ways can work be a privilege in my life?

A Virtuous Woman

Who can find a virtuous and capable wife?
She is worth more than precious rubies.
Proverbs 31:10

Every man is looking for a good wife, but this verse says that a virtuous wife is extremely rare—as rare as rubies. She is, in fact, far above rubies—she is priceless!

In Proverbs 31:10-32, we get a clue about this amazing woman's talents and priorities. Her responsibilities progressed from her husband, to her household, and then to the community. Her character was honest, reliable, and capable. The entire family benefited from her business enterprises. She was a real mover and shaker. She developed her talents. She was alert and alive. She prepared ahead for emergencies.

She worked willingly with her hands. In fact the word *hands* is used ten times in this chapter. She was physically involved in the process, probably ready to train, supervise, and patiently oversee the whole operation. Then we see her in the market shopping for the best buys. Smart homemakers have always done that.

This Proverbs 31 woman sounds a bit too good to be true, doesn't she? She can be intimidating, but don't let her be. As you seek to honor God with *your* unique talents and strengths, you, too, will become a woman of virtue and strength.

Making It Personal

What can I learn from this capable woman described in Proverbs?

Clothed with Kindness

She is clothed with strength and dignity. . . . When she speaks, her words are wise, and kindness is the rule when she gives instructions.
Proverbs 31:25-26

As we continue studying the Proverbs 31 woman, we read that she rose "before dawn" (verse 15). This woman had self-discipline and a servant's heart, which is one of the marks of a great leader. Not all of us are morning people, but early morning can be a great time to plan the day.

She was an executive in every sense. She made real estate deals, found bargains, and worked hard. Proverbs 31:18 says, "her lights burn late into the night." One Bible commentary I read suggested this phrase meant that a candle was left burning to show that their home was a place for the needy. Interesting thought. Always ready to help someone.

Along with everything else this lady had a first-class designer wardrobe. Her garments were regal and elaborately embroidered. But more important was the clothing of her heart. She was adorned inside with wisdom. Those who knew her best praised her for her kindness.

Though this woman is a perfect ideal no one can completely emulate, we can seek to clothe ourselves with kindness—a wardrobe that never goes out of fashion.

Making It Personal

How can I serve my family with kindness this week?

Lasting Beauty

Charm is deceptive, and beauty does not last; but a woman who fears the
LORD will be greatly praised. Reward her for all she has done.
Let her deeds publicly declare her praise.
Proverbs 31:30-31

Charm is cheap and beauty does not last. We all experience this every day. The older we get, the longer it takes us each day to make ourselves "presentable." No, we can't stop the aging process. No, beauty won't last. BUT, "a woman who fears the LORD will be greatly praised."

That is a powerful truth, isn't it? To "fear God" simply means to stand in awe of Him, revere Him, trust Him, humbly know He is God and we are not. When we do that, a new kind of beauty fills our hearts and spills out to others.

We can have all the abilities, all the energy, all the noble character traits of this woman, but God is looking for a woman of faith. He wants to write a new chapter of hope with our lives.

So pull out a "page" of your own life, a typical day. Write down everything you did from the time you got up until you went to bed. Review it and check the places where the woman of Proverbs 31 maybe would have acted differently given your circumstances. Are you a woman who fears and trusts the Lord?

Making It Personal

How am I investing in a spiritual beauty that won't fade?

Living to Serve

Work hard at living in peace with others.
1 Peter 3:11

We live in a world of complex relationships that challenge us daily. In particular, our relationships with our colleagues can be difficult at times.

We must remember that God calls us first to be servants. When I think of service to others, I remember Dorcas in Acts 9 who served and cooked for the poor widows and orphans of Joppa. In Acts 16, we read about Lydia—a career woman. She opened her home to those in need and she witnessed daily to her business associates of her faith in Christ.

These are wonderful examples of women being used for God's glory as they use their gifts. We can only be at our best when we fit into God's plan for our lives and serve others—even when it's difficult.

Making It Personal

When is it most difficult for me to serve others? Why?

August 22

Made for a Purpose

The LORD will fulfill his purpose for me.
Psalm 138:8 (NIV)

You may know the story of Susanna Wesley, the mother of John and Charles Wesley, the brothers who began the Methodist movement. John once wrote, "I learned more about Christianity from my mother than from all the theologians of England."

Susanna is a wonderful example of how God can use us right where we are. She was disciplined. She carefully structured her day so her children would have a routine. She was disciplined in training her children, going over and over academic and spiritual lessons. Susanna was also disciplined in her private devotional life—consistent and constant. I'm sure Susanna Wesley had difficult days, but she remembered that God made her for a purpose.

God calls us to have that kind of confidence. Those difficult days when the baby is crying for no reason, when the computer crashes again, when the five-year-old spills milk for the nineteenth time that day, when the meeting doesn't go well, when the sixteen-year-old calls, "Mom, I hit the garage door with the car!" All of these events contribute to the purpose to which we are called, shaping and refining us.

Making It Personal

When things go wrong, what can I do to remember that God will fulfill His purpose for me?

Back to Basics

So, you see, it is impossible to please God without faith.
Anyone who wants to come to him must believe that there is a God
and that he rewards those who sincerely seek him.
Hebrews 11:6

After a particularly crushing defeat to an inferior team, the great football coach Vince Lombardi called a practice the very next morning. Gritting his teeth, Lombardi began to speak: "This morning, we go back to the basics." Holding a football high enough for all to see, he yelled out, "Gentlemen, this is a football."

How basic can you get? That was like saying: "Librarian, this is a book," or "Marine, this is a rifle." He was talking to men who knew offensive and defensive plays in their sleep. Well, it worked. Going back to the basics enabled Coach Lombardi to lead his team to three consecutive world championships—something no one else has ever done.

What works in the game of football works in our spiritual lives as well. What is the most basic building block of our relationship with God? *Faith.* Faith overcomes failure. Faith overcomes fear. Faith overcomes doubts. Faith overcomes lack of self-esteem.

Faith means believing in advance what will only make sense in reverse. When we ask God for faith, He will give it. Sometimes we just need to get back to basics.

Making It Personal

What would it look like for me to have more faith in God today?

A Good Filter

Those who listen to instruction will prosper;
those who trust the LORD will be happy.
Proverbs 16:20

I don't drink coffee, which is probably why I don't make good coffee. Over the years, I have made coffee in the morning and watched my husband pour a cup, barely take a sip, and then set it down. I go back and check the amount of coffee I put in, check the water level, check the on/off switch, and finally I check the filter. Most of the time everything was all right—except that filter. A clogged and messy filter does not help my coffee-making abilities! A messy coffee filter is a sign that a change is needed. Cleaning up is in order.

Let's look at the filters in our professional lives. If you are beginning a business or going forward with a renewed vision, start by making sure your vision "filter" is cleaned out and can function. What does this filter do? It sifts out everything that is not absolutely essential. It repels false ideas and allows the proper vision and plan to pass through.

God's viewpoint is the best filter for life. When our plans and decisions pass through His loving hands, we know the result will be good!

Making It Personal

How can I make sure my business decisions
pass through God's filter first?

Never a Failure

You encourage me by giving me the strength I need.
Psalm 138:3

A re you feeling like a failure this week? Maybe you are in debt. Maybe a project you'd planned fell through, or a meeting you led didn't go well. Maybe you haven't been faithful to your employees or respectful of your supervisor. Maybe you've been so focused on profit that you have neglected your family relationships.

There are many events in life that cause us to believe we are a nobody. So I want to tell you something: *you are a somebody!* You may have failed, but you are not a failure. Failure is only temporary. It does not define you. Right now is the time to begin again!

You have lives to enrich. You have a job to pay your bills. You have a God who promises to never leave you. Start with what you have. Failure will pass, but faith is eternal!

Making It Personal

What things in my life are making me feel like a failure?
What can I do right now to begin again?

Give a Smile

A glad heart makes a happy face; a broken heart crushes the spirit.
Proverbs 15:13

The simplest personal touch is offering a warm smile. We can all smile. In fact, it takes fewer muscles to smile than to frown. The medical profession has long realized that happy people are the healthiest people.

We know from Nehemiah 8:10 that "'the joy of the Lord is [our] strength." Happiness passes; joy is something that abides. Happiness is a choice; joy comes from a relationship with the Lord. If we have joy, we are able to choose to be happy. Joy experienced should also be joy expressed—through a smile.

Elton Roth was assisting with evangelistic meetings in Texas on a hot summer day in 1923, when the words and music of a new song came to him. No matter the oppressive heat, his heart was filled with joy as he wrote:

In my heart there rings a melody,
There rings a melody with heaven's harmony.
In my heart there rings a melody,
There rings a melody of love.

Do you really want to make a difference in other people's lives? Then add that personal touch that comes from a joyful heart. Smile!

Making It Personal

What is in my heart today that is showing on my face?

Faith Beyond Logic

*One day the widow of one of Elisha's fellow prophets
came to Elisha and cried out to him.*
2 Kings 4:1

In the Old Testament we read about a widow who went to the prophet Elisha for help. She was in trouble with one of her late husband's creditors, who was threatening to take her two sons into slavery.

First, Elisha sent her to get pots from her neighbors. I wonder if the widow thought, *What are my neighbors going to think? What if Elisha's plan doesn't work out?* But she did what Elisha told her to do.

Doing what God asks us to do is not always the easiest thing to do—and it is not always the logical thing to do. What if this woman had tried to be logical? She could have said, "Elisha, why can't you just give me the money to pay off my debts and let me live in peace?" But if she had questioned, she would be robbing God of His glory! And she would not have seen the miracle of God's provision.

Making It Personal

**What step of faith do I need to take today,
even though it seems illogical?**

Little Is Much

"Tell me, what do you have in the house?" [Elisha asked].
"Nothing at all, except a flask of olive oil," she replied.
2 Kings 4:2

When the needy widow came to the prophet Elisha for help, Elisha started right in her own home with her own possession—a little flask of oil. He told her to pour oil into her neighbors' pots, beginning with the small amount of oil that she owned.

The widow poured and filled one pot full. Two pots full. And another and another. She did not stop pouring until all the jars were filled—a miracle! I can just imagine how excited she must have been. Each drop of oil meant her debt was being paid. Each drop meant food, clothing, life.

This widow was willing to take the one thing she had in her possession and use it for God's glory and for her good. Little is much when God is in it. Why are we so slow to believe it?

Making It Personal

What little bit of skill or possession do I have that
God might want to use for His glory?

A Big God

*By his mighty power at work within us, [God] is able to accomplish
infinitely more than we would ever dare to ask or hope.*
Ephesians 3:20

I saw a cartoon once that showed what the world looks like to a toddler. Chairs and tables were as big as skyscrapers, the family car was the size of a bear, and all the adults in the picture were shown only from the knee down. That is an interesting glimpse of what it's like when you're very, very small and everything around you is very, very big.

Some days are like that even for adults. We find ourselves "under the pile." We feel very, very small, as though everything in our lives is just too big for us to handle. Yet God is very, very big—bigger than any need we have. "Now glory be to God! By his mighty power at work within us, he is able to accomplish infinitely more than we would ever dare to ask or hope" (Ephesians 3:20-21). So look up!

Making It Personal

How big is my view of God?

What God Hates

There are six things the LORD hates—no, seven things he detests.
Proverbs 6:16

Apart of wisdom is realizing what God hates as well as what He is pleased with. Proverbs tells us seven things that displease God.

1. *Haughty eyes.* Haughtiness comes from feeling superior to others. It is the opposite of a serving nature.
2. *A lying tongue.* Truth telling is a part of personal integrity and a vital part of team performance.
3. *Hands that kill the innocent.* This is usually related to violence, but Jesus equated anger with murder (Matthew 5:21-22).
4. *A heart that plots evil.* Not many people would confess to this wrong, but any time we gossip, we are plotting evil.
5. *Feet that race to do wrong.* When people do not have a good value system, they become eager to lie, cheat, deceive, and steal.
6. *A false witness who pours out lies.* The telling of lies and half-truths is rampant in the media, school textbooks, and particularly business.
7. *A person who sows discord among brothers.* We are to be in the business of building people up, not tearing them down.

Do we really believe what God says about the things He hates? If so, let us act that way.

Making It Personal

As I look at my life, do I find any of the things God hates?

A Work in Progress

*God, who began the good work within you, will
continue his work until it is finally finished.*
Philippians 1:6

I believe God is sovereign, and so I believe He will finish the work He has begun in me. I believe that is true for you, too. There's just no getting away from Philippians 1:6: "I am sure that God, who began the good work within you, will continue his work until it is finally finished on that day."

I am sure that God has worked, is working, and will continue to work in our lives. He will never quit. We are His work in progress.

Does that mean we should sit back and expect God to do everything? Of course not! We continue doing what we know to do: meet the needs of people, honor the Lord, and strive to improve in our work. But at the same time, we keep looking with faith to see what God is up to in our lives.

Making It Personal

What do I see God doing in my life and labors?

September

Fall is when school begins, leaves turn to gold, and things start hopping. Make this season a productive, busy time.

With love
Joan

Batter Up!

The reward of the godly will last.
Proverbs 11:18

I n one *Peanuts*® cartoon, Charlie Brown lamented the fact
that we're all thrown into life too fast, and so we're just
not prepared. Linus replied, "Well, what did you want—a
chance to warm up first?"

We've all been thrown into the game of life and we
have to play. As a matter of fact, your business is a lot like a
baseball game. You have a season ahead of you—that's the
chance to make good in your work. You have a "bat"—the
product or service your company sells. The "balls" are your
customers. Selling is like getting a hit in the big game. Just
as in baseball, we need those hits to keep things going!

Baseball players train every year. They must be ready
to react instantly, whether on defense or offense. They
have to hit the ball, run, throw the ball, and catch the ball.
Likewise, you need to hone many business skills and be
ready for changes on the job.

If you practice hard, learn everything you can from
"coaches," and work faithfully as a team member, you will
succeed.

Making It Personal

Ready or not, how can I make myself a star player in my business?

Thankful No Matter What

*No matter what happens, always be thankful, for this is
God's will for you who belong to Christ Jesus.*
1 Thessalonians 5:18

If you have small children, you know how hard you work to teach them to say "Please, Mommy" and "Thank you." When they actually say it without your prompting, it just melts your heart, doesn't it? If we're that way as human beings, how much more must God be overjoyed when one of His children responds to His goodness with a thankful heart!

Paul's advice for us is to be thankful for everything, no matter what has happened. That means being thankful for everything from the littlest to the biggest blessing. That means making thanksgiving a part of our lifestyle.

What makes us thankful? It isn't our circumstances or what's in our bank account, but what's in our heart.

Making It Personal

What am I grateful for? How will I thank God?

A Name, Not a Number

[A shepherd] calls his own sheep by name and leads them out.
John 10:3

The business world can be a cold and impersonal environment. Especially in larger corporations, we can feel like an unknown part of a big machine—that's the downside of getting big!

With so many computers spitting out numbers these days—credit card numbers, account numbers, and many more—it is very difficult to keep it personal. When you are born, you are given a Social Security number that identifies you for your whole life. Yet making a person into a mere number is dehumanizing. I don't want to be a number; I want to be Joan. We are all persons, not numbers. The Bible tells us that Jesus, the Great Shepherd, knows each of His sheep by name. Isn't that awesome!

Let's work harder to learn people's names. Let's give them the personal touch we long for ourselves.

Making It Personal
Who will I call by name today?

Free to Work

Those who work hard will prosper and be satisfied.
Proverbs 13:4

L abor Day is a reminder to all of us of the privilege it is to work in the greatest country in the world. Other places in the world have unsettled conditions, wars and strife, and hurting people. We are so blessed to live in the United States, still the land of the free. We are free to start a business, free to select a product and sell it, free to work in a clean, comfortable environment, free to enjoy new friendships at our workplace.

Freedom is such a blessing for all Americans. Why do people from around the world risk their lives to come to live and work in America? It is for freedom, which is not free by any means. A very dear price has been paid by many people to preserve our freedom.

So on this Labor Day, I am grateful I can work. I am grateful for the faithfulness of so many hard working staff in our business. I pray we will never forget the freedom and privilege we have to work.

Making It Personal

What aspects of my job do I really enjoy?

Dainty Morsels

What dainty morsels rumors are—but they sink deep into one's heart.
Proverbs 26:22

What truth this proverb offers! It's so easy to share private information about someone else, thinking it will do no damage. But a small comment here or there can cause great harm in the workplace.

I cannot emphasize this enough: Do not spread gossip. Do not participate in gossip. Who do you think is really hurt by gossip? *You are* if you pass it on. Don't even listen in on gossip. Stop it in midstream by asking, "May I quote you?" If the answer is no, then tell the person not to repeat any more.

Gossip—those dainty morsels—has the potential to destroy both business and personal relationships.

Making It Personal

In what ways do I contribute to gossip?

September 6

Loving Service

You have been called to live in freedom—not freedom to satisfy
your sinful nature, but freedom to serve one another in love.
Galatians 5:13

We've all experienced service without love. Clerks at the grocery store checking us out grumpily. Waiters in restaurants taking our order rudely. Shoe sales ladies finding our size of shoes to try on, but obviously not happy with their work. They really don't care about the customer. Oh yes, they are serving us, but without any love or care for us.

The great Green Bay Packers' coach Vince Lombardi was known as a strict taskmaster who had many championship teams. Yet he once said that his team's success was due to the fact that they loved each other. Even though these guys were tough players, they loved each other!

Let's add to our service an extra ingredient: love. Let's serve with a genuine smile that says, "You are loved." What a difference we can make!

Making It Personal

How can I revolutionize my service through love?

Solid Hope

*So I pray that God, who gives you hope, will keep you
happy and full of peace as you believe in him.*
Romans 15:13

We use the word *hope* every day, yet many people don't really have it. Hope is the feeling that what we desire will happen. The Spanish word for *hope* is "esperar," which means "to wait for or to expect." To hope, then, also has an element of waiting for something to happen, of anticipating it.

Hope is kind of like faith—it's not how much you have, but what you put your faith *in* that counts. The Bible links hope with faith, and tells us that hope is "the confident assurance that what we hope for is *going to happen*" (Hebrews 11:1).

I think many of us separate hope from its real source. The truth is that the source of true hope is not found in our own dreams and wishes coming true, but is found in God's promises that will never fail.

Making It Personal

What is the source of my hope?

September 8

Servant Leaders

Whoever wants to be a leader among you must be your servant.
Matthew 20:26

The most important quality of leadership is found in Matthew 20:26: "Whoever wants to be a leader among you must be your servant." Good leaders have a servant's heart. They know that people are their most important asset. They work hard at making other people successful. They aren't puffed up about themselves. Instead, they emphasize the achievements of others.

Sometimes people with big titles think they are better than others—they think they have arrived and that they are automatically leaders because of the title behind their name. A title is no guarantee of real leadership. Regardless of a title, a leader is someone who influences others through strength and character.

Leadership is not a right, it is a responsibility. Serving the interests of those who follow is true leadership.

Making It Personal

How can I build up someone else today?

Home Building

A house is built by wisdom and becomes strong through good sense. Through knowledge its rooms are filled with all sorts of precious riches and valuables.
Proverbs 24:3-4 (*Verse of the Year 1990*)

I have a real burden for women who are desperately trying to balance their family life with their business. Each person who comes into Premier has a different need and a different environment in her home. But every woman must strive to have a healthy balance. What to do? These two verses in Proverbs tell us how to build a solid home:

- By wisdom: seeing with discernment; the ability to sense what is beneath the surface.

- By good sense: weighing things with perspective.

- By knowledge: learning with perception, having a teachable spirit, a willingness to listen to find out what is really there.

In Proverbs 24:3 the word for *built* comes from the Hebrew term that suggests "to restore." It is the idea of rebuilding something so that it flourishes again. Ask God for wisdom, good sense, and knowledge to know how to restore and build something good at home.

Making It Personal

In what ways do I need to restore and build up my home life?

September 10

Being Available

A house is built by wisdom and becomes strong through good sense.
Proverbs 24:3

Let's look at Proverbs 24:3 again. Wisdom is putting our knowledge into action. If you are frustrated in trying to find balance between your work and home life, here are some suggestions to consider.

1. Close your office during meals. This means no telephone calls. Tell people you will return calls promptly, as you have free time.

2. Be available when your children come in from school. Sit down with them, if only for fifteen minutes. That is priority! I was so privileged to be able to be there for my kids, and hear them call out, "Mom, I'm home!" There's not a sound like it anywhere!

3. Be available for your spouse. Plan a date night or a date breakfast. Commit to time alone together. Lord willing, your lives together will extend many years beyond the child-rearing time, so don't neglect your relationship and cherish each hour you have together.

4. Have a family outing at least once a month. Have fun together! And as the children grow older, include them in discussions of how to balance your time. You might be surprised at their wisdom.

Making It Personal

Which of these steps, or others, do I need to take to keep balance in my home?

A Day to Remember

I will fear no evil, for you are with me.
Psalm 23:4 (NIV)

September 11, 2001, changed our world forever. Even now, remembering that awful day of terrorism can bring feelings of fear, discouragement, and uncertainty. Instead of growing anxious, though, I suggest we *remember*. Remember those who paid the ultimate price for freedom. Remember the families who lost loved ones.

Then *pray*. Pray for our country, for our president, and for his cabinet of advisers. Pray for those in the military and their families left behind. Pray for those working to keep our country safe. Pray for our enemies.

Most important, let's give thanks to God. We don't have to fear, knowing that God is in control of the affairs of this world. Though we face many unknowns, His promises will never fail.

Making It Personal

How can I rest in God's peace even in uncertain times?

Team Building

*How wonderful it is, how pleasant, when
brothers live together in harmony!*
Psalm 133:1

A large part of building a solid business is putting together a great team. John Stemmons, a well-known Dallas businessman, said this about building a team: "Find some people who are 'comers,' who are going to be achievers in their own field, and who are people you can trust. Then grow old together."

As the word *comers* implies, these are people who haven't arrived yet. Comers are on the go and on the grow. They are willing to work diligently. Comers are also destined to achieve "in their own field." That is crucial. After all, a team can't possibly be made up of all quarterbacks or all running backs.

The key to your team—or any team you will build in the future—is that you have different members who are all comers and all achievers. They are all working for a common goal. You can trust all of them completely.

It is thrilling to see how God puts together a team and uses them. So let's have that team spirit!

Making It Personal

Who might God want on my team?

A Word of Wisdom

*The LORD was pleased with Solomon's reply and
was glad that he had asked for wisdom.*
1 Kings 3:10

God appeared to Solomon in a dream and told him to ask for anything he wanted. Solomon could have asked for riches, for land, for power. But he prayed for wisdom. (What would you and I have asked for, I wonder?)

One aspect of wisdom is the ability to see life from God's perspective. For example, some people think it's wise to climb to the top of the corporate ladder, but God's wisdom says if you want to be great, you must be a servant. Another aspect of wisdom is common sense, the ability to use knowledge to come to correct conclusions. Solomon used his common sense when he dealt with the two women who were fighting over one baby (1 Kings 3:16-28).

Because Solomon asked for something that would benefit others, God granted his request and also blessed him with great wealth and power. This does not mean that we will automatically make millions if we follow Solomon's example, but the principle remains true. God is waiting to bless us abundantly if we strive to please Him.

Ask for real wisdom in running your business, and watch in amazement as God blesses it.

Making It Personal

What do my prayers reflect about my desires?

Are You a Procrastinator?

*Don't brag about tomorrow, since you don't
know what the day will bring.*
Proverbs 27:1

Procrastination isn't all it's cracked up to be. To procrastinate, Mr. Webster says, is "to put off intentionally and habitually postpone; to put off reprehensibly the doing of something that should be done." *Reprehensible* is pretty strong language. When we procrastinate, we say "later" or "tomorrow." In reality we're saying, "Who cares if it ever gets done?"

Why do we become procrastinators in our work? I have come up with two reasons why we delay and postpone.

1. We have no goals in mind or down on paper. We look at our work as a hobby that we can pick up at will or that we can stuff in the closet when it interferes with our short-term fun.

2. Or we do have goals, but we have set goals that are unrealistic. Then, when we miss these goals, we become sad and frustrated.

Don't let procrastination pull you down. Set realistic goals and go after them.

Making It Personal

What realistic goal can I get started on today?

The Most Admirable Quality

*Good people are guided by their honesty; treacherous people
are destroyed by their dishonesty.*
Proverbs 11:3

At the University of Santa Clara in California, a researcher conducted a study of fifteen hundred business managers, asking them what they value most in a boss. What do you think the researcher discovered?

Employees said they respect a leader who (1) shows competence, (2) has the ability to inspire workers, and (3) is skillful in providing direction. And indeed, all three qualities are very admirable.

But there was a fourth quality the workers admired even more: *integrity*. Above all else, the workers wanted a manager whose word is good, who is known for honesty, and whom they can trust.

If I were to ask you the same question that the researcher asked, what would be your reply? Do you, yourself, embody the admired qualities, especially integrity? Integrity should characterize all of us, no matter what our position.

Making It Personal

How much do I value integrity in my life? In other people's lives?

God's Values

Who may worship in your sanctuary, LORD?
Who may enter your presence on your holy hill?
Psalm 15:1

Psalm 15 describes the character of a person who can enter God's sanctuary. These questions in Psalm 15:1 are answered in the following verses by an elevenfold description of the "righteous" person—one who lives by God's values.

1. She is blameless.
2. She does right.
3. She speaks the truth.
4. She won't slander.
5. She doesn't harm others.
6. She doesn't speak evil of others.
7. She despises persistent sinners.
8. She honors the Lord's followers.
9. She keeps her promise.
10. She doesn't charge interest.
11. She doesn't accept bribes.

We can appreciate these virtues. But we also know that if anyone tries to live a good life on his or her own, it can be a constant uphill battle. We need God's help, and must moment by moment live under the control of the Holy Spirit. "Such people will stand firm forever" (Psalm 15:5).

Making It Personal

How does this list reveal the things that God values?

September 17

String of Pearls?

The twelve gates were made of pearls—each gate from a single pearl!
Revelation 21:21

Did you know that the lovely pearl is a product of pain? For some unknown reason, the shell of an oyster gets pricked and an alien substance—a grain of sand—slips inside. Upon the entry of that irritant, all the resources within the sensitive oyster rush to the spot and begin to release healing fluids. By and by, the irritant is covered and the wound is healed—by a pearl.

No other gem has so fascinating a natural history. The pearl is the symbol of stress, a healed wound, a precious jewel conceived through irritation. There could have been no pearl if there had been no wounding in the first place.

Some oysters are never wounded. And what happens to these? They are tossed aside, fit only for oyster stew.

We all have had an irritant slip inside our hearts for some unknown reason, and when that irritant becomes recognized, all the resources within us rush to that spot of pain. What happens then determines whether we will have a string of pearls or merely oyster stew.

Making It Personal
What irritant is creating a potential pearl in my life right now?

September 18

Say It Again

Having carefully investigated all of these accounts from the beginning, I have decided to write a careful summary for you, to reassure you of the truth of all you were taught.

Luke 1:3-4

When we've been in a business for a while, it's easy to think that we've heard it all before. We get bored because the information we are receiving seems repetitious. Why go to the weekly staff meeting when we know it all already? Why attend another rally or training event when we've been before?

The author of the Gospel of Luke admitted that many other people had written accounts of Jesus (Luke 1:1-2), so why did he bother to check the information for himself? Because he wanted to reassure his readers of the truths they had heard. The fact that others had written the story of Jesus did not hinder Luke from taking up the pen and writing it again. I am so glad he didn't mind saying things over in a new way.

Let's not be too proud to pay attention when we hear the Philosophy, Purpose, and Plan of our company repeated over and over. It reminds us and reassures us of the core values of enriching lives and serving others.

Making It Personal

What messages do I need to hear over and over?

Passing the Blame

"The serpent tricked me," she replied. "That's why I ate it."
Genesis 3:13

What does it mean to be responsible? To be responsible means we are "answerable" and "accountable" for our actions. Irresponsible behavior is nothing but immaturity. Being responsible is a sign of maturity—not necessarily in years, but in behavior.

A good example of immaturity and irresponsibility is found in the Bible story of the first family. God told Adam and Eve they could eat of any fruit of the garden, except from one tree. But the woman was tempted and ate from that tree. She coaxed her husband to eat also. When God asked them what had happened, Adam laid the responsibility for his disobedience on Eve. An immature Eve, in turn, blamed the serpent for her sin.

It's a very human trait to pass the blame. Rarely will we stand up and admit a mistake, although we are quick to claim the credit when things go well. Responsible people can own up to their own actions.

Making It Personal

Are there any mistakes I need to own up to today?

Fall Produce

*The more you grow like this, the more you will become productive
and useful in your knowledge of our Lord Jesus Christ.*
2 Peter 1:8

The autumn season is awesome. The colors of the leaves and the temperature changes energize us after the lazy, hot days of summer. School begins, apples ripen, and things start hopping. Fall can be a productive, busy time.

Deborah was a woman in the Bible who was busy and productive. She made the most of her opportunities. (You can read her story in Judges 4:1-24.) She was a colorful leader who had strength of character. But her real strength was her complete trust in God.

I see other traits in Deborah's "fall colors" of leadership. She was decisive; she made her decisions quickly and she didn't change them. And she was effective in delegating what needed to be done.

In our Premier business, fall is often the time of greatest opportunity. It may be our busiest season. Like Deborah, you will have many decisions to make. Learn how to make good, solid decisions. You will also have more than you can do. Learn how to be a person who can delegate, so your business will be well tended in this busy season.

Making It Personal

Am I a good decision-maker?

Attitude of Encouragement

Then they stood on each side, holding up his hands until sunset.
Exodus 17:12

In Exodus 17, we read that the Amalekites attacked the Israelites at Rephidim. Moses instructed Joshua, his follower, to go to battle. As Joshua fought, Moses stood at the top of a hill and held up the staff of God. "As long as Moses held up the staff with his hands, the Israelites had the advantage. But whenever he lowered his hands, the Amalekites gained the upper hand" (17:11).

Moses was doing his job as a leader, but he grew weary. Eventually, his arms were too tired to hold up the staff. So Aaron and Hur put a stone under him and he sat down. Then Aaron and Hur "stood on each side, holding up his hands until sunset" (17:12). And Joshua and the Israelites won the battle.

Imagine yourself in that scene. It shows what our attitude should be toward our leaders. Sometimes we forget that they need affirmation and help just as we do! We are to *encourage* those who lead us. An attitude of encouragement towards leadership will help make a whole company strong.

Making It Personal

How can I encourage a leader or mentor in my life?

The Joy of Trouble

*Dear brothers and sisters, whenever trouble comes
your way, let it be an opportunity for joy.*
James 1:2

Make a mental list of things that irritate you. Here are suggestions to get you started: traffic jams, talkative people, long lines, crying babies, misplaced keys, stuck zippers, deadlines, noisy neighbors, late planes, tight clothes, flat tires, slow delivery of merchandise. Any of those get you uptight?

If it weren't for interruptions, we'd have no problem being patient, would we? Unfortunately, life isn't like that. There will never be freedom from irritations—never! So then, the secret is that we must adjust. Sounds simple, but it isn't. Through adjustments we experience inner growth. "When your faith is tested, your endurance has a chance to grow. So let it grow, for when your endurance is fully developed, you will be strong in character and ready for anything" (James 1:3).

It is possible to endure adversity and come out the winner. Adversity is a good test of our ability to cope, to stand back up, to recover from misfortune. And through the adjustments we make, we will become spiritually mature.

Making It Personal

When have I seen problems in my life strengthen my character?

How to Keep Your Honey

*A worthy wife is her husband's joy and crown;
a shameful wife saps his strength.*
Proverbs 12:4

Competition is good. It motivates us, generates new ideas, and offers challenges. But we must avoid selfish competitiveness. If our motive is to always beat out someone else, it is unhealthy.

Being successful in your business can be a great blessing. Just be aware that an unhealthy competition between a husband and wife about who makes the most money can sometimes threaten a marriage. Take the time to talk these matters over together. Determine how you will balance the rewards of your business with the needs of your marriage.

Keeping your honey is your number-one job. Fortunately, honey is sticky! Make your honey stick to you and you stick to him.

Making It Personal

What effect is my work having on my marriage?

Training Manual

*Train up a child in the way he should go, and
when he is old he will not depart from it.*
Proverbs 22:6 (NKJV)

Training is a major part of every business. So let's look
at Proverbs 22:6 from that perspective.

First, the word translated "train up" was used for
bringing a wild horse into submission by a rope in the
mouth. I doubt that our coworkers are like wild horses,
but you never know!

Second, the word "child" in ancient times was applied
to infants up through children of marriageable age. This
suggests that we always need to be learning, throughout
our career, no matter what our age.

Third, the phrase "in the way he should go" refers
to showing a child how to employ natural gifts and
abilities in the right way. Applied to business, this means
we should teach Jewelers the correct procedures and
guidelines, and then let them be their own persons as they
implement them.

I realize that I have taken liberties in applying this
verse to training in business. But good training is tremen-
dously important. The groundwork you lay in training
others will be invaluable to your business.

Making It Personal

What insight from Proverbs 22:6 is most helpful to me in training?

Refiner's Fire

He will sit and judge like a refiner of silver,
watching closely as the dross is burned away.
Malachi 3:3

A goldsmith sat on the floor by his crucible, working on gold. He was asked, "How long does it take for it to be purified?"

"Until you can see your face in it," he replied.

God, too, is a refiner—a refiner of His people. "He will sit and judge like a refiner of silver, watching closely as the dross is burned away" (Malachi 3:3). He wants to see His image in us, and so He refines us through our struggles.

Hardly a life is lived without experiencing some tragedy. The French have a saying for this: *C'est la vie!*— That's life! Christ has a more encouraging word for us: "My gracious favor is all you need. My power works best in your weakness" (2 Corinthians 12:9).

Yet God places our faith in the crucible of testing. Why? To prove it is genuine. Gold is refined in the fire, and our faith is more valuable than gold (1 Peter 1:7).

Job knew about tragedy and testing. He lost everything he had and everyone he loved. But he had faith that when his testing was finished, he would "come forth as gold" (Job 23:10 NKJV). May the same be true of us.

Making It Personal

What good things have I learned through struggles in my life?

September 26

Jump-Start Encouragement

There was Joseph, the one the apostles nicknamed Barnabas (which means "Son of Encouragement").
Acts 4:36

Encouraging someone is like giving a dead battery a jump-start with jumper cables. It transfers strength from one to another. In the Bible, one awesome example of an encourager is Barnabas. He was a true motivator. We find his story in the book of Acts.

Barnabas was a landowner from Cyprus and he was probably a wealthy man. The apostles changed his name from Joseph to *Barnabas*, which means "son of encouragement." We would probably call him Mr. Encouragement.

We don't know exactly how Barnabas encouraged others, but we do know some things about him. For example, he "was a good man, full of the Holy Spirit and strong in faith" (Acts 11:24). He is also given as the example of early Christians who generously shared their goods with the needy (4:32-37).

Barnabas wasn't just talking the talk; he was walking the walk. That's how we really motivate and encourage others. We transfer our strength to others, not so much by our words, but first and foremost by "doing" it.

Making It Personal

How can I encourage others with my actions?

Encouraging Potential

Barnabas took John Mark with him and sailed for Cyprus.
Acts 15:39

Someone asked Winston Churchill, "What in your school experience best prepared you to lead Britain out of her darkest hour?"

Churchill thought about it a moment and said, "It was the two years I spent at the same level in high school."

"Did you fail?"

"Oh no. I had two opportunities to get it right."

It's obvious Churchill was raised with encouragement. We need to encourage people who are in need, but we can also encourage those who have potential. Barnabas did the same. After John Mark abandoned Paul and Barnabas, Barnabas wanted to accept him back (Acts 13:13; 15:36-39). The "son of encouragement" didn't focus on Mark's problems; he saw his potential and found a way to encourage him.

We all can look for potential. That probably means we will defend the underdog and love the unlovely. Nevertheless, we always should look for a spark we can fan into a flame.

Making It Personal

Whose potential can I encourage today?

Holding Back

[Ananias] sold some property. He brought part of the money to the apostles, but he claimed it was the full amount.
Acts 5:1-2

In the book of Acts we read the story of the beginning of the Christian church. At first, these new Christ-followers lived in community, and many of them gave of their worldly goods to support those who needed it. Ananias and his wife, Sapphira, wanted to contribute, so Ananias sold some property and "brought part of the money to the apostles, but he claimed it was the full amount" (Acts 5:2).

Compare what Ananias did with what Barnabas, the encourager, did: "[Barnabas] sold a field he owned and brought the money to the apostles for those in need" (Acts 4:37). What a contrast! Ananias said the right words, but he was holding back, not being sincere. Barnabas gave it all, keeping back nothing for himself. Barnabas was a genuine giver, whereas Ananias wanted the recognition but was dishonest and unwilling to pay the price up front.

We can't expect a blessing for ourselves or for others if we are not honest about our efforts. We can't be true motivators or encouragers like Barnabas until we give of ourselves freely and with no obligation. We need to be sincere and not just give lip service to encouraging others. Remember, flowery words blow away like the breeze.

Making It Personal

As an encourager, am I willing to give myself freely or do I hold back?

Riding Third Class

Share each other's troubles and problems,
and in this way obey the law of Christ.
Galatians 6:2

When taking a stagecoach in the old West, there were three types of tickets a passenger could purchase: first-class, second-class, and third-class.

If you were a first-class ticket holder, you could ride inside the coach. If something went wrong—say, a wheel came off or the coach got stuck in the mud—you would remain in the coach until the problem was fixed.

If you were a second-class ticket holder, you also rode inside the coach, but if a problem developed, you were required to get off until the problem was solved. You could stand in the distance and, if you desired, lend advice that might help to solve the problem.

If, however, you were a third-class ticket holder, you rode inside the coach only if there was room, and if a problem developed, you had to get off and help fix it. This could mean holding the coach up while the wheel was fixed, or pushing the coach out of the mud.

Which ticket holder do you resemble when problems arise in your company? I hope you're not too proud to be like the third-class ticket holder and get down in the mud to help fix the problem!

Making It Personal

Am I a willing helper in times of difficulty?

Rest

*Lord, doesn't it seem unfair to you that my
sister just sits here while I do all the work?*
Luke 10:40

Do you ever feel like you're on a treadmill—always moving but not going anywhere? We get busy, and then we get burned out. Jesus' friend Martha was busy preparing a meal for several guests. She worked and worked, all the while resenting her sister, Mary, who was sitting and listening to Jesus.

The lesson from the story of Mary and Martha is not that work is wrong. After all, God put the first man in the Garden of Eden and told him to work it (Genesis 2:15). God worked hard Himself at Creation, and we're not told that He had coffee breaks or stopped to watch the Super Bowl. But when He was done, He rested (Genesis 2:2). And He expects us to rest, too.

One of the Ten Commandments addresses this issue: "Six days a week are set apart for your daily duties and regular work, but the seventh day is a day of rest dedicated to the Lord your God" (Exodus 20:9-10). And as my pastor used to say, these are the Ten Commandments, not the Ten Suggestions!

Work is a large part of our life, but God intends us to rest some. He does not want our work to become a snare to us.

Making It Personal

Do I have the right balance of work and rest in my life?

October

When we serve others, we are serving the Lord.

With love,
Joan

October 1

The Personal Treatment

*When you did it to one of the least of these my brothers
and sisters, you were doing it to me!*
Matthew 25:40

God has blessed me with many sweet and dear friends. I want to be involved in their lives as much as time allows me. I want to encourage them, show love and concern, be a friend to those who need me, write personal notes, and just be there for them.

Whatever I can do, my commitment is to keep it personal. It makes a difference to treat others that way, and it makes a difference to be treated that way. I don't really notice if Neiman Marcus thanks me in a form letter for using their credit card. I do notice when I receive a personal thank-you note from the salesclerk named Marie who sold me the hosiery at Neiman Marcus. She didn't have to do that, but how much that meant to me!

That is the personal touch. And when we serve others, we are serving the Lord.

Making It Personal

How can I give some personal treatment to a friend today?

Margin of Victory

Do you see any truly competent workers?
They will serve kings rather than ordinary people.
Proverbs 22:29

At the end of the baseball season, do you know how many hits separate a .290 batter from someone who averages .300? It's not a hundred hits. It's not even fifty hits. It's only *five* additional hits. That is less than one extra hit per month for six months. What a difference that one hit can make!

Success is often measured by slim margins. In baseball, it's just one more run, just one less strike, or just one more walk. In business, it can be just one more phone call, just one more meeting, or just one more clinched sale. Accomplish that "one more" and you can move up to the major leagues!

We don't win every day. Sometimes we strike out. In business, our game might be rained out today—but tomorrow there may be sunshine!

The timing for your big wins is not entirely in your control—it depends on many things. Ultimately God is in control. He knows what is best and when it is best. Our part is to work on improving our batting average one hit at a time.

Making It Personal

How can I improve my "batting average" this week? This month?

October 3

Lord of the Sea

*Who else has held the oceans in his hand? Who has measured off the
heavens with his fingers? Who else knows the weight of the earth
or has weighed out the mountains and the hills?*

Isaiah 40:12

The ocean reminds me of how much we need God's
provision. We are far more dependent on the sea than
we realize. It seems that history has always been tied to
sea power and waterways. Even in ancient times, whoever
dominated a major waterway held a key to power.

And these powerful waters were created by an all-
powerful God! When I watch the ocean, I see God's mighty
hand always moving. The Bible tells us that God has held
the ocean in His hand, has measured the heavens, and
has weighed the earth. We can only use poetic language
to describe the mighty God we have!

Sometimes when we read the newspaper headlines or
listen to "Gloom Time" news on television, we can lose
sight of the fact that God is in control. But as I reflect on
the vast oceans and our dependence on them, I remember
how big God is and that He provides for us. He only asks
us to depend on Him.

Making It Personal

What other parts of nature show me God's awesome power?

The Goal of Satisfaction

*I decided there is nothing better than to enjoy food
and drink and to find satisfaction in work.*
Ecclesiastes 2:24

Fall is in the air. It's time to rake leaves and clean out yards. The squirrels gather food, getting ready for winter. I hope you have been raking up knowledge and inspiration and storing it away to use over and over. You may need to commit to a fresh start with new goals, not the old leaves of bad habits hanging around.

You have the freedom to set your own goals, say, to be the best businesswoman you can possibly be. From then on, that goal will control your behavior and choices. Let me suggest another worthy goal to you. The wise man who wrote the book of Ecclesiastes said there is nothing better to do than to "enjoy food and drink and to find satisfaction in work." Are you really satisfied with your daily life? In your work? If not, set some new goals to learn what it means to be satisfied in these areas.

We cannot change yesterday nor begin tomorrow until it is here. So all that is left is to make today the best it can be and be satisfied with that.

Making It Personal

How can I find more satisfaction in my work?

Happy to Serve

*I know all the things you do—your love, your faith,
your service, and your patient endurance. And I can see your
constant improvement in all these things.*
Revelation 2:19

Market research confirms that the salesperson is more important to the customer than the product. In our business, it goes without saying that selling yourself comes first. And that begins with building a relationship of trust.

Of course, many factors contribute to building trust. The most important one is service, service, service. My husband, Andy, has said over and over, "You can sell without serving, but you can't serve without selling." A servant attitude, more than any other trait, makes our selling productive. It also brings us much joy in the process.

Albert Schweitzer was a man with a servant's heart. He said, "The only ones among us who will really be happy are those who have sought and found how to serve." Happiness is a byproduct of service and a job well done.

Making It Personal

How can I unite service and selling in my work?

Gentle Words

*But the wisdom that comes from heaven is first of all pure. It is also
peace loving, gentle at all times, and willing to yield to others.*
James 3:17

When we show anger, irritation, impatience, stress, or guilt, we very often say words that are anything but kind. This is when we really need help from the Lord to control our tongues.

Ask God to help you control your tongue. Ask Him to help you speak with kindness and gentleness. And ask Him for wisdom.

James 3:17 tells us: "The wisdom that comes from heaven is first of all pure. It is also peace loving, gentle at all times, and willing to yield to others. It is full of mercy and good deeds. It shows no partiality and is always sincere." If wisdom is peace loving, gentle, merciful, and sincere, then we need a lot of wisdom to speak kindly! And if kindness, gentleness, and peace control our tongues, then we will be worth listening to.

Making It Personal

How can I remember to speak with gentle wisdom?

October 7

A Difficult Assignment

*If we don't love people we can see, how can we
love God, whom we have not seen?*
1 John 4:20

There was a missionary teacher in Africa who encouraged her students to love others, but she struggled to get along with an impossible coworker. Finally, an elderly African woman challenged her, pointing out that she was not showing the love that she was teaching.

What an embarrassing blow that must have been. But the missionary was not to be defeated. She determined that for one year, every day, she would read the "love chapter"— 1 Corinthians 13—and live with those verses fresh on her mind as she carried out her daily tasks. It became a pattern that changed the course of her life. People began to notice amazing changes not only in the missionary's life but also in the other "difficult" coworker's life as well.

It's easy to love people who love us, but what about that critical person in your family or that nosy neighbor? What about a coworker who pushes all your buttons? Perhaps you are dealing with this kind of situation right now. What a difference it can make in our dealings with difficult people if we would just read and follow the wisdom of the God's Word!

Making It Personal

*Is there a difficult relationship in my life right now?
How can I love that person?*

Against All Hope

*Hope deferred makes the heart sick,
but when dreams come true, there is life and joy.*
Proverbs 13:12

The Bible records a wonderful story of hope and dreams coming true. Abraham and Sarah were very old, long past the childbearing age and long past any hope of heirs. But God promised that they would have a child. Sarah laughed as she thought, *How could a worn-out woman like me have a baby?*

Years went by. "Hope deferred makes the heart sick." They could have found many reasons to give up.

"I'm too old."

"Nothing like this has happened before."

"We've tried for years and it hasn't worked."

Their only hope was to believe God's promise. Romans 4:18 (NIV) tells us that "against all hope, Abraham, in hope, believed." And their faith was rewarded. Twenty-six years later, God intervened and a son was born! Sarah declared, "God has brought me laughter! All who hear about this will laugh with me. For who would have dreamed that I would ever have a baby?" (Genesis 21:6-7).

When dreams come true, there is life and joy. The Lord had the last laugh, reminding them, "Is anything too hard for the Lord?" (Genesis 18:14).

Making It Personal

What are some of my dreams and hopes? How can I trust God as I wait?

October 9

Celebrity or Servant?

Whoever wants to be a leader among you must be your servant.
Matthew 20:26

Astronaut James Irwin had an interesting insight while his spacecraft was hurtling back to earth. He recalled, "As I was returning to earth, I realized that I was a servant, not a celebrity. So I am here as God's servant on planet Earth to share what I have experienced, that others might know the glory of God."

Becoming a leader in a company does not make you a celebrity. Rather, it makes you a servant. And the higher you go in leadership, the more of a servant you are.

More than any other trait, a servant attitude makes for a productive leader. It will take precedence over personality, skill, and education. Skills can be taught, education can be achieved, but a servant attitude is a matter of the heart and comes from the core of a person. A servant leader will always be thinking, *What can I do for others?* not *What is in it for me?* or *How can I show them I am in control?*

As you think about advancing in your career, are you prepared to be a servant?

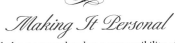

Making It Personal

How do I feel about servanthood as a responsibility of leadership?

Abilities at Work

*To those who use well what they are given, even more will
be given, and they will have an abundance.*
Matthew 25:29

Deep within everyone is a desire to do great things.
But to carry out our desires, we need the means.
These means are our abilities or talents—the gifts God has
given to each of us.

You have the opportunity to discover your own
abilities and use them. And if you are leading a team of
people, you also have the exciting opportunity to discover
the abilities or gifts of each person you supervise.

As you meet together for training, you can spot gifts as
they rise to the surface. Not everyone is gifted in teaching
or training, but Jodi may be creative and can add to your
team in that area. While you may not have an aptitude for
detail, you may have observed that Susie is detail-oriented.
Take advantage of her abilities.

As a leader, observe and encourage the abilities that
God has given each person on your team—and be thankful
for them. Matthew 25:29 says that if we will use wisely
what we have, we will be given more.

Making It Personal

What abilities does each person on my work team possess?

A Worthy Goal

Learn to be wise, and develop good judgment.
Don't forget or turn away from my words.
Proverbs 4:5

What are your goals in life? Happiness? Financial security? Peace and joy? To be a good wife, a great mom? The Bible tells us that one of our goals should be learning to be wise. Easy to say, hard to do.

What is wisdom? I read this definition somewhere: *Wisdom is the ability to meet each situation with discernment and good judgment.*

Having knowledge is not the same as having wisdom. If we have the knowledge and don't act upon it, it's the same as not knowing at all. Wisdom involves using the knowledge we have to take the proper course of action. The true test of wisdom is knowing how and when to act, according to God's will.

Charles Haddon Spurgeon, a well-known nineteenth-century preacher, put it this way, "Wisdom is the right use of knowledge. To know is not to be wise, but to know how to use knowledge is to have wisdom." Let's make it our goal to learn to be wise.

Making It Personal

How do I define wisdom?

The Gift of Time

There is a time for everything.
Ecclesiastes 3:1

Have you ever spoken to someone who is looking to the side as you talk, or even looking right at you but not really listening? We all need to work on this.

Give time to your husband when he is speaking. Ask him to give you that gift in return. Listening, giving attention, spending time together—what a gift! This time doesn't have to be an hour or a day. It can be very precious when it is just two minutes of undivided attention.

And what about your children? You're being pulled in so many directions already, and then your kids demand your attention. You may be tempted to say, "I don't have time for you right now!" How much better to give yourself to them for just a few seconds—if that's all you have then—and acknowledge that need for attention.

Then there are some colleagues or neighbors who may talk your ear off. Is it possible they just need attention? They may need some of your valuable time. What a wonderful gift to give them. Not all of your time, but some!

If we commit this gift of our time to our family, to colleagues, to our neighbors, it will help them know that they are special.

Making It Personal

Who can I surprise with extra attention this week?

October 13

Encouragement as a Lifestyle

*Let's return to each city where we previously preached the
word of the Lord, to see how the new believers are getting along.*
Acts 15:36

Encouragement is not a one-time event; it's a commitment for a lifetime. That's how Barnabas looked at it. He and Paul returned to people they had already met with to encourage them some more. That's a lesson for us: We encourage again and again. We don't quit. We are there for people.

Now sometimes we need to receive encouragement ourselves, right? And that's good. But don't use that as an excuse to stop reaching out. From the examples in the Bible and from human experience, we can understand that God places a high priority on encouragement. Encouragers care about people, and encouraging is a lifestyle for them.

To be an encourager will cost us time and will not always be easy. People don't seem to have crises at convenient times. We have to care enough to encourage others in a personal, loving way no matter what the schedule.

Making It Personal

*How can I make giving encouragement not a
one-time event, but a lifestyle?*

How May I Serve You—Better?

*Don't get tired of doing what is good. Don't get discouraged and give up,
for we will reap a harvest of blessing at the appropriate time.*
Galatians 6:9

In a cute *Peanuts*® cartoon Charlie Brown asked Lucy why we are here on this earth. Lucy answered that we're here to serve other people. Charlie asked, "Well, then, why are other people here on earth?"

The answer, of course, is that we are here to serve *one another.* The noun *servant* and the verb *serve* are found about 500 times in the Bible. If nothing else, that emphasis should encourage us to be servants!

There is much written these days about service. Improving customer service is the challenge for many businesses. That's why the bottom line (as the corporate world puts it), or the starting point (as I prefer to call it), is not "How may I serve you?" but "How may I serve you *better*?" We must have a serving spirit that comes through in all areas of our business. And our commitment must be to constantly renew and upgrade our service to others.

Making It Personal

Is there room for improvement in my service to others?

October 15

Doing Good

[Dorcas] was always doing kind things for others and helping the poor.
Acts 9:36

I receive many letters nearly every week from people in our business. They often write about a member of our company who had a setback in business or a life-threatening illness. Then they tell how there was someone from our company who did kind things and stepped in to help where needed.

It's not always easy, and it's not always convenient, but it's always good to do good! The old preacher John Wesley said it this way: "Do all the good you can, in all the ways you can, to all the souls you can, in every place you can, as long as ever you can."

Dorcas was a woman in the New Testament who had quite a reputation for doing good. Wouldn't it be special if we could be remembered, as Dorcas was, for doing kind things and helping the poor?

Making It Personal
To whom can I be a Dorcas and do good?

The Narrow Truth

The gateway to life is small, and the road is narrow,
and only a few ever find it.
Matthew 7:14

These days it is popular to criticize biblical truth as being "narrow." But as my pastor used to say, all truth is narrow. Scientific truth is narrow. Mathematical truth is narrow. Geographical truth is narrow.

If you have a thousand-dollar note due at the bank, you can't go to the banker with $900 and say, "I want to pay off my loan."

The banker will reply, "That is not enough."

You might think, *Well, how narrow!* But that doesn't change the facts, does it?

One winter morning, I talked on the phone to our daughter and grandchildren in Bolivia. They were preparing to go swimming. You see, it was summertime there. In Dallas that morning, though, it was 41 degrees, and the facts dictated that I should not go swimming. Was I being narrow? The freezing water would probably have given me a heart attack. That was the narrow truth.

All of these illustrations point out one glowing fact: truth is narrow but not ever confining. God's truth makes us free! Seek to follow His truth in all things.

Making It Personal

What "narrow" truth is God calling me to obey?

Make a Date

She carefully watches all that goes on in her household.
Proverbs 31:27

In the midst of deadlines, phone calls, and e-mails, it helps to have a plan in place for spending quality time with our kids. One suggestion is to have a calendar just for your children. Keep it in a special place—maybe the kitchen where they congregate after school.

When the children come home from school or other activities, ask them to put down any special events coming up that they really want you to attend. It will take some time to develop this habit, but believe me, it is worth a ton of diamonds.

If your children are very young, with no outside activities, make a "date time" with them and put it on their calendar. Maybe go out for breakfast or to a park for lunch.

One other word about this: Try to separate yourself from that telephone when the children arrive home. Give them the courtesy of your attention. It is a good plan to shut it off during mealtimes as well. And when you make a date for special time with your children, keep it! You'll be surprised at the joy that time brings.

Making It Personal

What can I do to help a child feel special today?

Back to Stage One

*Go back to what you heard and believed at first;
hold to it firmly and turn to me again.*
Revelation 3:3

Every career goes through different stages. First there is the *creative stage*. This is when we have a dream and are filled with excitement and enthusiasm. We want to learn everything. We are busy building the business and overcoming obstacles. We have pride and momentum.

When things begin to go well and smooth out, the second stage begins: *management*. This is when we are focused on orderly planning and managing. After all, our business cannot survive on enthusiasm alone. But sometimes we get so bogged down in managing things that we forget our purpose.

Then comes the third stage, best described as the *defensive stage*, when we begin rationalizing our behaviors that are causing problems. If we don't control our defensiveness, we can easily move into the fourth stage: *blaming*. Instead of taking responsibility for our mistakes, we blame family, friends, associates, lack of money, lack of time, the economy—anybody and anything but ourselves.

But don't lose heart. No matter what stage you may find yourself in, God is a God of new beginnings. We can always go back to stage one and renew our excitement!

Making It Personal

What stage is my career in?

The Lord's Delight

*Let not . . . the rich man [boast] in his riches. Let them
boast in this alone: that they truly know me.*
Jeremiah 9:23-24

Perhaps you have had a promotion recently or received an award for achievement. Maybe you have reached a point in your career where you are well-off financially. Can you boast about that? No! Bragging about our paychecks, new homes, or expensive cars doesn't impress the Lord.

What does God delight in? That we truly know Him and understand that He is the Lord who is just and righteous, whose love is unfailing. There's absolutely nothing we can *do* that will impress God. But we can be holy. We can be in love with the Lord. We can seek to know Him and *understand* Him. That pleases Him.

The older I get and the longer I walk with the Lord, the more I realize that I serve a God who doesn't need my help, my ideas, or my plans. But rather, as today's verses say, the Lord values our desire to understand and know Him.

Making It Personal

How can I make knowing God a priority in my life?

Everlasting Love

I have loved you, my people, with an everlasting love.
With unfailing love I have drawn you to myself.
Jeremiah 31:3

We all have broken relationships of one kind or another. But a broken relationship with our heavenly Father is the most grievous of all. We are separated from Him because of our sin. God is perfect, just, and righteous, and He cannot look on my sin or your sin.

But He also is a loving Father. He has loved us with an everlasting love and has made a way out for us. He wanted to have fellowship with us, so He gave the only perfect sacrifice that would pay the price for our sin: the death of His Son.

I remember well the Sunday in 1951 when I made the decision to accept this free gift of salvation. I was very aware of my sin and guilt, and I felt dirty before God. But when my heart cried out, "Yes, Lord," I felt cleansed. I knew God's everlasting love was for me.

Deciding what you believe about Jesus Christ is the most important turning point in anyone's life. More important than becoming marketing director or sales-person of the year. More important than becoming president and CEO. When we decide to follow Christ, God's everlasting love really comes home to us personally.

Making It Personal

Do I know God's everlasting love and forgiveness of my sin through Christ?

October 21

Don't Stay in Neutral

Watch out, so that you do not lose the prize for which we have been working so hard. Be diligent so that you will receive your full reward.
2 John 1:8

When it comes to your career, which gear are you in? If you're in first gear, at least you're moving forward. Second gear is better, and third or fourth gear is better yet. I hope you're not in park or reverse!

But there's another gear that I want to warn you about: neutral. Putting a career in neutral is not stopping it, as with park, nor living in the past, as with reverse. But it is not powering ahead, either. Neutral is where you take everything for granted. You begin to assume that all is going great, but in reality you are just coasting. Have you ever left your car in neutral and it still moved? Yes, it will move, but the movement will all be downhill!

Have you been impressed to make some changes in your life or in your business, but have done nothing? As my friend Mary Crowley used to say, "Impression without expression brings depression." Don't drop into neutral. Get going!

Making It Personal

Am I living in neutral? How do I shift into a higher gear?

Set Your Sail

You will keep on guiding me with your counsel,
leading me to a glorious destiny.
Psalm 73:24

Picture yourself as a sailboat. Before you can have clear sailing in your life and your business, you must consider such factors as the wind, the clouds, and the water.

The movement of the air propels a sailboat along, and likewise the "wind" in our lives is anything that advances our careers. This can be a success on the job, a promotion, or whatever.

When you're out on a sailboat and you see clouds gathering, you have to decide whether you should head for shore or go on. Similarly, we can encounter "clouds" of discouragement or "storms" of disappointment that hinder reaching our goals. Again, we must make a decision.

The water a boat sails on can offer calm seas or choppy waves, but you have no choice but to sail whatever kind of water you're on. We have in our careers various conditions—good or bad—that we must "sail" over to get to our destination.

But there is one more factor to consider. All sailboats have a rudder, and the rudder determines what direction the boat will go. In the same way, if God is directing our lives, we will go wherever God will receive the most glory.

Making It Personal

How is my "sailing" journey going? What direction is my boat going?

Plug-In Drug

This is the day the LORD has made. We will rejoice and be glad in it.
Psalm 118:24

Ninety-seven percent of American homes have television sets. That is a larger number than homes that have indoor plumbing. The *Christian Medical Society Journal* once commented, "The primary danger of the television screen lies not so much in the behavior it produces, as the behavior it prevents."

I like that. We may not be watching bad shows, but think of all the things we could be doing instead of watching television. Reading. Writing. Thinking creatively about a business challenge. Enjoying a few restful moments alone. Just plain conversing with family and friends. So many people and tasks fill our days that we need to be aware of the things that sap our hours.

Television has been called the plug-in drug. But it's not the TV itself that is so paralyzing; it is the overuse of it when we could be doing something else that truly enriches our lives.

Making It Personal

What could I do with my few extra minutes today instead of watching television?

20/20 Vision

Then Jesus told him, "I have come to give sight to the blind and to show those who think they see that they are blind."
John 9:39

Did you know that you blink about twenty-five times every minute? Each blink takes about one-fifth of a second. If you take a ten-hour automobile trip and average forty miles per hour, you will drive twenty miles of that trip with your eyes closed! Can you believe that?

More surprising than that trivia fact is that some people go through their whole lives with their eyes closed, so to speak. They look but don't really see. They look at people but don't see their needs or envision how to serve.

I also know many wonderful people who see more than those who have 20/20 vision. They have insight and discernment. They are perceptive enough to see beyond the obvious.

I pray that we will use our eyes to really see, so we can be helpful to those in need.

Making It Personal

Who is one person whose needs I could better "see" today?

The Power of Commitment

Commit your work to the LORD, and then your plans will succeed.
Proverbs 16:3

When my son Tim played football in high school, he went to practice every morning before school and stayed late at practice every night. During the grueling "two-a-days" in August before school started, he practiced four hours in the morning and four hours in the evening. His team went over and over the same plays, the same drills, the same defenses. Many days he would come home too exhausted to eat.

Why did he get up the next day and go back at it? He was committed to it! He never would have endured the mental and physical stress if he hadn't believed in the coach's plan. And the hard work paid off when the real games began.

So why do you keep learning at work, even when you are tired of the training? Because you are committed to the Philosophy, Purpose, and Plan of our business. Training isn't always easy. But if you believe in what you're training for, you will stay committed until the end.

Making It Personal

What level of commitment do I have to my business?

Credibility

*Do not merely listen to the word, and
so deceive yourselves. Do what it says.*
James 1:22 (NIV)

When you are training others, whether employees or a new colleague, remember that you need to establish credibility if the training is to be successful. You need to be sure you and your trainees are on the same wavelength. The person you are training will learn better if she trusts you and believes in what you are teaching.

That means you need to believe in it! That belief includes going out and doing what you're talking about. How would it look if you instructed someone how to do a task, and then you turned around and did it in a completely different way, or didn't do it at all? Remember that one of the keys to successful training is establishing credibility.

Making It Personal

Do I have credibility with the people I work with?

October 27

Encouragement by Letter

*There was great joy throughout the church that day
as they read this encouraging message.*
Acts 15:31

In his book *Loving God*, Chuck Colson tells the story of an old woman, named Grandma Howell, who was sick, lonely, and depressed. She began to believe she had nothing left to live for. Then God said three words to her: "Write to prisoners."

In the years remaining to her, Grandma Howell wrote hundreds of letters to prisoners. But that was only half her joy. They wrote back and made her last years the most fulfilling of her life.

There is incredible power in encouraging letters and there is also great joy. I can personally relate to that, both the giving and the receiving. The price of a stamp has changed, but the need for encouraging notes has not. Written encouragement conveys a thoughtful investment of time.

I am a great proponent of handwritten notes, but I realize that technology does make it possible to save time in writing. So whether our notes are handwritten or computer-driven, we all can encourage others by the written word.

Making It Personal

To whom will I write an encouraging note today?

On the Menu

*You will have all the food you want, and you
will will praise the LORD your God.*
Joel 2:26

I hope you are hungry today, because I want to focus on food. Let's look at the connection between a menu and your business.

- *Appetizers.* Yummy snacks that get you started. Getting new products, receiving training, meeting coworkers—these are some of the things that form the foundation of your work and whet your appetite for success.

- *Entrée.* The entrée is the main course. Our entrée is our main approach to work, made up of six ingredients: (1) consistency, (2) reputation, (3) dependability, (4) motivation, (5) excellence, and (6) service, service, and service!

- *Dessert.* The finishing touch of a meal. Our dessert is comprised of the sweet extra rewards we receive. These can include bonuses, rewards, recognition, and promotion.

The best way to enjoy a good meal is to appreciate each course. The same is true in your business.

Making It Personal

Do I have a balanced business in all these areas?

October 29

Ingredients of Business Success

*So make every effort to apply the benefits of these promises to your life.
Then your faith will produce a life of moral excellence.*
2 Peter 1:5

Yesterday, we briefly noted the six ingredients to the "entrée" of business success. Today, I want to examine those ingredients more closely.

1. *Consistency.* For example, figure out how many sales opportunities you can handle without jeopardizing your family life, then do that number every month.

2. *Reputation.* Remember that you represent your company. So tell the truth and keep a positive attitude.

3. *Dependability.* Do what you say you will do when you say you will do it.

4. *Motivation.* Attend gatherings designed to pump up the employees of your company. Read inspirational books.

5. *Commitment to excellence.* Do not be satisfied with mediocrity. Strive for excellence.

6. *Dedication to service.* This should be our hallmark as Christian women in business—being committed to always asking, "How may I serve you?"

To keep your business strong, don't leave out any of these recommended ingredients.

Making It Personal

Is my work made up of the right ingredients?

Always Accountable

Fools think they need no advice, but the wise listen to others.
Proverbs 12:15

You have probably known people who don't feel that they are accountable to anyone. This is a dangerous place to be. I believe it is very profitable for each of us to find someone to whom we are accountable.

Proverbs 12:15 says that fools think they need no advice, but the wise listen to others! Listening to others and even accepting constructive criticism requires humility. Being vulnerable and real with someone you can trust is essential to personal growth. Pray that God will lead you to a mature godly person to fill the role of mentor and leader in your life.

We are never beyond needing accountability in our business lives or personal lives. I have two very special godly friends I depend on to keep me in line and to pray for me. Don't forget the importance of depending on others.

Making It Personal

Do I accept help or constructive criticism easily? Why or why not?

A Real Mentor

Don't let anyone think less of you because you are young.
Be an example to all believers.
1 Timothy 4:12

Think for a minute about the people who have had the most positive impact on your life. How did they influence you? Why did they make such an impression?

I imagine that those who have influenced you the most took the time to be involved in your life. They cared about you as a person and were vulnerable enough to share their own lives with you.

Sometimes we think mentoring is only when an older person helps a younger person succeed. That may be the usual situation. But I am here to tell you that many young people have had a great impact on me. They have significantly influenced the way I act, how I speak, and how I care for my appearance. As they influence me, I, in turn, desire to influence others. That's being a role model—that is mentoring.

Making It Personal

Who has been a true mentor in my life? Why?

November

What makes us thankful?
Knowing that God is in
control, and that He is
loving and good.

With love
Joan

Ready to Serve

Do for others as you would like them to do for you.
Luke 6:31

How many times have we said, "That service is terrible!" Good service is often sacrificed for speed. Cashiers are in such a hurry that they don't take time to be polite. Clerks are rude or unhelpful. Phone calls are put on hold for far too long. Manufacturers are not willing to fix what they sell. All these things not only show a lack of service, they also show a lack of interest in serving. Many companies have forgotten what it means to truly serve one another.

When you call in to our company, hearing that voice on the other end saying, "Good morning, how may I serve you?" really starts your day on a high note, doesn't it? We are prompted to be ready to serve.

The good news is that in an impersonal world, the way you do business can stand apart. You have the opportunity to surprise people with how well you care for them. It is difficult to measure service, but one of the best ways to recognize it is to see that customers value a product more because the people behind the product genuinely care.

Making It Personal

*In what specific way can I surprise someone with a
positive attitude toward serving?*

Pleasing Words

*May the words of my mouth and the thoughts of my heart
be pleasing to you, O LORD, my rock and Redeemer*
Psalm 19:14

We try to impress upon all who are in our business that they represent the company. You are Premier Designs. I am Premier Designs. Everything we say and do reflects negatively or positively on the company as a whole. This is especially true of what we say. Often our words are remembered long after our actions are forgotten. If our thoughts and meditations are acceptable to God, then our words will please Him also.

Jesus said, "Whatever is in your heart determines what you say" (Luke 6:45). In other words, what is in the well of your heart comes up in the bucket of your speech. In Proverbs 25:11 (NIV) we read, "A word aptly spoken is like apples of gold in settings of silver." (I'm sure the gold and silver is a reference to Premier jewelry, don't you think?) So watch your words. If it is not true or apt or meaningful, it is best not to express it.

Making It Personal

How can I make my words pleasing and acceptable today?

Love in Action

*Dear children, let us stop just saying we love each other;
let us really show it by our actions.*
1 John 3:18

*L*ove—that powerful word—is both a noun and a verb. I'd like to focus on *love* as a verb.

"Love is something you do" an old song observed. More than just words, real love is action. More than just a deep feeling, real love is doing. Love is desiring the best for someone else.

The Bible tells us that God is love. God's love is a verb: He showed His love by giving His Son. He first loved us, undeserving as we are. Isn't that amazing? If God can love us, then we need to learn to love each other. We cannot love perfectly as God does, but we can try.

Love must be in our hearts for it to come out in our behavior. I truly desire that my friends, family, and work family will see my love for them by my actions. Above all, I want God to be pleased. May we each share more, serve more, do love more.

Making It Personal

How can I act out love toward someone today?

Shepherding

The LORD is my shepherd; I have everything I need.
Psalm 23:1

On our trips to Israel, Andy and I have enjoyed watching the shepherds on the hills with their sheep. I heard that sheep do not take care of themselves; they require more human assistance than any other class of livestock. The shepherd, then, provides a marvelous example of patient care for his flock.

The Bible says a lot about God being our Shepherd. Perhaps the most familiar passage is Psalm 23. Take some time to read through this beautiful psalm. Now I don't want to be accused of heresy, because I know this psalm contains deep spiritual truths. But I want to use it loosely as an analogy and say that any leader in business is like a shepherd. Looking at Psalm 23:1 in that light, we see that the welfare of a "flock" is entirely dependent upon the "shepherds" in management.

A good shepherd goes to no end of trouble to supply his sheep with the finest grazing, food, and clean water. We, too, will have to do whatever it takes to meet the many needs of those we are responsible for at work.

Strive to be a good "shepherd" on the job. What a responsibility and what a marvelous opportunity!

Making It Personal

What more do I learn from Psalm 23?

Hungry Sheep

He lets me rest in green meadows; he leads me beside peaceful streams.
Psalm 23:2

David, the author of Psalm 23, herded his own sheep on the dry and dusty hills of the Holy Land. There, green meadows and pastures do not just happen by chance, but are produced with much labor and skill. The shepherds have to clear the rocky land, tear out roots and stumps, plant seeds, and then irrigate with water. They do a tremendous amount of work in order that their sheep can enjoy green pastures. They know those pastures are necessary to the survival of the sheep.

There is no substitute for providing good pasturage. Hungry sheep are always on the move, looking to satisfy their gnawing hunger. Without food, they will end up lying down, losing all their vigor and vitality. They can even die.

What a helpful metaphor this is. Some of our co-workers may be dissatisfied and discouraged. Some may be ready to lie down and die in their business. Provide some green pastures: spend time with them, keep your promises, give them training and information they need to fulfill their potential. Do whatever it takes to help them, not just to survive but to thrive.

Making It Personal

How can I help someone else who may be discouraged?

Fearful Sheep

I will not be afraid, for you are close beside me.
Psalm 23:4

Ever come upon some sheep on a narrow road out in the country? In a situation like that they all scramble, the ones at the back panicking and pushing the others. Sheep are so timid and easily panicked, in fact, that even a stray jackrabbit suddenly bounding from behind a bush can stampede a whole flock. When one startled sheep runs in fear, a dozen others will blindly follow.

A flock that is restless, discontented, always agitated and disturbed never does well. In order for the sheep to lie down contented, they must be free from fear.

The same is true for us. Human beings can be very fear-driven. Generally, it is the unknown that produces the greatest uneasiness. When we are fearful, we are unable to cope with the little tests that come our way. But remember that we have a good Shepherd! He is always close beside us. We don't have to fear.

Making It Personal

What fears are building up in my life that I need to let the Shepherd handle?

Worry or Trust

Martha was worrying over the big dinner she was preparing.
Luke 10:40

I can just hear Martha saying, "Well, I would love to sit around and listen to Jesus, but after all, someone has to do the work. This dinner isn't going to prepare itself!" She was a worrier. I know how she felt, because I can be a worrier myself. I have even discovered that the more I worry about being busy, the busier I become, because then I'm worrying about not being busy enough!

But Jesus, in effect, said to Martha (and maybe to me and you, too), "You are a wonderful worker, but you are also a wonderful worrier. Don't worry about things that must get done. You'll burn out and then you won't have time for fellowship with Me."

We all have a choice. We can worry and let all that busyness interfere with our work, or we can let God control our time and get more done.

How do we trade worry for trust? One key is to set aside time each day to be still before God in prayer and reading the Bible. Some people find that "quiet time" first thing in the morning. Others may be able to be quiet with God later in the day. We need to listen with our hearts as God speaks to us through His Word—then believe what He tells us.

Making It Personal

How can I turn away from worry and turn toward God?

Priorities

"Martha, Martha," the Lord answered, "you are worried and upset about many things, but only one thing is needed. Mary has chosen what is better, and it will not be taken away from her."
Luke 10:41-42 (NIV)

Martha was busy preparing the big meal and she wanted Jesus to notice all she was doing and to thank her for those efforts. Jesus did notice, but He had no praise for her. Instead, he gave her a gentle reminder that she was not taking care of priorities. There were more important things to do right then than cook dinner.

What sort of work was Martha doing—was it bad? No. She was busy serving. It wasn't a question of good or bad; it was a question of better or best. Mary chose the best part—sitting at the feet of Jesus.

In the same way, we need to get our priorities in order if we are going to control our busyness. Good things often crowd out more important things. By overdoing, we sometimes have no time or energy left to do the most necessary work. We overdo until we are done in. Then we become irritable and unhappy.

When you are overloaded and overdoing, will you stay busy, or will you choose the better way?

Making It Personal

Are my priorities the best ones?

Fly, Run, Walk

But those who wait on the LORD will find new strength. They will fly high on wings like eagles. They will run and not grow weary. They will walk and not faint.
Isaiah 40:31

This is one of my favorite verses because it is such a wonderful promise. Those who wait on God will be renewed! They will first fly, then run, then walk—the opposite of what we usually think. We would put walking first, then running, and finally flying. But when we wait on the Lord, we have complete confidence in Him. We are able to walk steadily without growing weary.

I am going to add something else to waiting: *sitting.* Waiting on the Lord means sitting still sometimes, being quiet and listening. Our trust and confidence is built as we wait, watch, sit, and listen. As God leads us, our faith is strengthened.

Soon after I became a Christian, I was given a book entitled *Sit, Walk and Stand* by Watchman Nee. I learned that to really make my life count for the Lord, I must sit at His feet each day before I walked out into the world. It was then I could stand tall.

Remember the importance of slowing down with God, taking the time to sit and listen.

Making It Personal

How can I fly, run, walk, and "sit" with God today?

Are You Available?

Teach us to make the most of our time, so that we may grow in wisdom.
Psalm 90:12

If you really want to make a difference in people's lives, you need to develop genuine relationships. Of course, it is impossible to be deeply involved in the lives of everyone you know. But you can select a few people you want to influence and encourage. Then, take the initiative. They will not normally seek you out, so you must be proactive.

Next, make yourself available. Your influence will be in direct proportion to your availability. And availability requires time.

I can hear you saying, "I'm too busy already." I know the problem intimately! I also know from personal experience that my schedule needs to be trimmed and rearranged from time to time. This frees me up to invest my time more wisely and devote myself to the areas where I can have the greatest impact. Giving of our time will have the greatest impact on those we serve.

Making It Personal

Who will I take time to help or influence today?

November 11

The Cost of Freedom

Give thanks to the LORD and proclaim his greatness.
Let the whole world know what he has done.
Psalm 105:1 *(Verse of the Year 2001)*

When I was in high school during World War II, there were very few boys my age left in our town. They were fighting for our freedom in a foreign land—with your grandfathers, dads, brothers, and uncles. Many, many of these heroes never returned to us. I can vividly remember losing very close friends. Freedom is not free; sometimes it costs life itself.

Many are paying a price today for the fight against terrorism around the world. Our heroic military men and women have proudly represented America in its time of need for decades. How do we respond to their sacrifice? We will "give thanks to the LORD and proclaim his greatness." We will "let the whole world know what he has done." For God has given us uncounted blessings. Freedom to work, to enrich lives, and to honor Him. Freedom to develop our own businesses. Freedom to vote our conscience. Freedom to worship as we please.

On Veteran's Day, let us remember that these are all gifts from the Lord, bought and protected by American veterans.

Making It Personal

What freedoms can I thank God for right now?

Celebrating Differences

*There are different ways God works in our lives,
but it is the same God who does the work through all of us.*
1 Corinthians 12:6

To be successful in the workplace you must appreciate your employees, coworkers, and supervisors for who they are—not for who you want them to be. This can be frustrating when you and a coworker have a different communication style, or when you wish your supervisor was available more often. There's a lot you can't change about your work environment. It may help to remember that others might want to change some things about you, too!

Each of us has different gifts and strengths. When we recognize and celebrate those gifts, we are more likely to see what others do offer rather than what they don't offer.

I believe that when we seek out the good in each other, we can understand that even with all our differences, we are all here to make a difference—to enrich the lives of those we touch.

Making It Personal

What are the strengths of one person I tend to disagree with?

November 13

Slowing Down

In quietness and confidence is your strength.
Isaiah 30:15

In the classic book *Alice in Wonderland*, the Red Queen tells Alice, "Here, it takes all the running you can do to keep in the same place. If you want to get somewhere else, you must run twice as fast."

That's true in our world, too, isn't it? We are rarely still. We're running around going forward or backward, and sometimes going nowhere. I wonder how much more we could accomplish, how many more people we could serve, if we took the time to be still every once in a while. We need to slow down and listen to God's direction, to see the needs of others, and to seek wisdom in how to respond to those needs.

It's true that running hard can be an important part of growing a business. We need to meet deadlines, respond to phone calls, and take care of emergencies that come up. But maybe we would be better prepared for that running if we took some time to be still first and find confidence and strength from God.

Making It Personal

How can I be still today?

Unbound

Lazarus came out, bound in graveclothes, his face wrapped in a headcloth.
Jesus told them, "Unwrap him and let him go!"
John 11:44

It was a thrilling moment. Jesus called to the dead man in the grave, and the man came walking out of the tomb, still wrapped in strips of cloth. Then Jesus commanded the onlookers, "Unwrap him and let him go!"

Jesus still frees us today. There are so many ways that He can unbind us and free us up. What about material needs? The single mom and others in economic trouble can be freed up financially as Christ gives them the strength to work and earn money.

What about self-confidence? The shy person who can't even lead in prayer can slowly begin to feel more confident and free from fear as Christ encourages her.

What about self-image? So many women have been told over and over again, "You can't do that." Can such a woman be unbound? Yes, she can. With Christ's resurrection power she can be a new person with a new identity.

If you feel bound up in some way, let Christ free you.

Making It Personal

What is one thing binding me up today?

Partnering with God

As God's partners, we beg you not to reject this
marvelous message of God's great kindness.
2 Corinthians 6:1

The apostle Paul called the believers God's partners". Think about that. We are all working with our heavenly Father, the omnipotent, omniscient, immutable God. Wow! What do you think we can contribute to the process? Are we really helping?

That reminds me of the time our daughter Sarah was young, and she wanted to help me sweep the kitchen floor. Normally, the sweeping would take me three or four minutes, but when little Sarah helped, it took a lot longer! I didn't mind, though, because she was helping and she did the best she could.

I wonder if that's how God looks at our helping. He doesn't need our help, any more than I needed Sarah's help in sweeping. But God graciously allows us to help in accomplishing His purpose and mission.

Making It Personal

What is God asking me to help Him accomplish?

Reasons for Joy

Those who have been ransomed by the LORD will return to Jerusalem, singing songs of everlasting joy.
Isaiah 51:11

There are countless reasons for us to be joyful. Let's see what God's Word says about this.

One reason for joy is forgiveness. "Purify me from my sins, and I will be clean; wash me, and I will be whiter than snow" (Psalm 51:7). On April 24, 1951, I understood that I needed forgiveness. When I confessed my sin, God forgave me and saved me. That's joy!

A second reason for joy is the promise of deliverance. "Those who have been ransomed by the Lord will return to Jerusalem, singing songs of everlasting joy. Sorrow and mourning will disappear, and they will be overcome with joy and gladness" (Isaiah 51:11). The prophet Isaiah was reminding Israel that God had not forgotten them in their days of suffering. He would rescue them.

A third reason for joy is having the Word of God. "Your words are what sustain me. They bring me great joy and are my heart's delight, for I bear your name, O LORD God Almighty" (Jeremiah 15:16). To read God's Word is to love it. So if you don't have joy, get in the Word. That's the cure!

Making It Personal

What is my number one reason for being joyful?

The Very Best

*The LORD says, "I will guide you along the best pathway
for your life. I will advise you and watch over you."*
Psalm 32:8

A little girl prayed, "God bless Mama and Papa, my brothers and sisters, and all my friends. And now, God, do take care of Yourself, for if anything should happen to You, we'd all be in the soup." How true that is! The little girl knew she needed God's guidance in life, just as we all do.

In *The Pursuit of Excellence,* Ted W. Engstrom writes about why some people excel and others don't. His principle is "just five minutes more." In other words, putting a mere five minutes of extra effort into something can make all the difference. For example, how about spending five minutes more per day asking God to give you the guidance you so desperately need?

David (the author of Psalm 32) was confident that God would do what He had said He would; that is, guide David along the best pathway for his life—the very best one! Are you confident that God will guide you into the very best if you ask Him? Believe it!

Making It Personal

How can I put the "five minutes more" principle into practice in my life?

My Purpose

Whatever you do, you must do all for the glory of God.
1 Corinthians 10:31

One of the books making the rounds today is *The Purpose-Driven Life*. It has caused many to reflect on, *What is the purpose of my life? Do I really make a difference? Or to put a different angle on it, If I belong to God, what does He want me to do with this life He has given me?*

I want to have a purpose in my life. Don't you? God's Word tells us how we can.

First Corinthians 10:31 informs us that everything we do is to be done for the glory of God. Does that really mean *everything*? Yes, everything. Ephesians 2:10 is one of my favorite verses. "We are God's masterpiece. He has created us anew in Christ Jesus, so that we can do the good things he planned for us long ago." So this is our purpose: to do the things God has planned for us. Simply put, our purpose is ministry.

The older I get, the more confident I am that God has designed a purpose for my life, and that through that purpose He will bring glory to Himself. The same is true for you.

Making It Personal

Specifically, what does God's purpose for my life look like?

Happy Planting!

You will always reap what you sow! . . . Those who live to please
the Spirit will harvest everlasting life from the Spirit.
Galatians 6:7-8

Have you ever thought of your life as a garden that may or may not bear fruit? Plant these rows of "vegetables" and you will have a productive garden.

Three rows of "lettuce;"
Let us be faithful.
Let us be loyal.
Let us love one another.

Three rows of "peas;"
Prayer
Preparation
Perseverance

Three rows of "squash;"
Squash gossip.
Squash criticism.
Squash indifference.

Three rows of "turnips;"
Turn up with a positive attitude.
Turn up with a smile.
Turn up with a thankful spirit.

Making It Personal

Which rows have I already planted in my life?
Which do I still need to plant?

God So Loved . . .

*God so loved the world that he gave his only Son, so that everyone
who believes in him will not perish but have eternal life.*
John 3:16

My dear friend Amy George, born in the Ukraine as Emma Wasylenko, spent several years in a German prisoner-of-war camp. She eventually made her way to Dallas, where she became a Christian. Meanwhile, she had lost contact with her father, Fyodor. But do you think God had lost contact with him? Certainly not!

Amy prayed for her father for many years. One night she received a call saying that he was in a New York airport, with a piece of paper that listed her name and address. She quickly made arrangements to bring Fyodor back to Dallas.

During the time Fyodor was in Dallas, Amy and her family told him about the Lord Jesus. Not many days passed before Fyodor accepted Christ as his Savior. He believed John 3:16 was true for him: "God so loved Fyodor that he gave his only Son, so that if Fyodor believed in him, Fyodor would not perish but have eternal life."

Was that an impossible happening? Not when you take into account the overwhelming love of God!

Making It Personal

When have I been overwhelmed with God's love?

November 21

The Heart of Business

Instead, be kind to each other, tenderhearted, forgiving one another,
just as God through Christ has forgiven you.
Ephesians 4:32

Your customer or client is the heart of your business. Never forget that! Customers come from all walks of life with varying needs, some carrying heavy burdens at times. What an opportunity! You can determine to serve them by speaking and living the truth always.

Be dependable and trustworthy. When you discover someone is hurting, tell them you care. Don't ask questions to be curious, just be ready to listen.

Show strength of character by rejecting anything that lowers your standards. Be pure, be honest, be generous. Generosity is important because, above all, generosity is an attitude. I'm not speaking of giving away the store—that's not necessary or wise. I am speaking of having a generous attitude toward others' shortcomings. Give them the benefit of the doubt.

Remember, customers are not dependent on you; you are dependent on them. It is your privilege to serve them.

Making It Personal

How can I develop a more generous attitude toward my customers?

Keys to the Job

*So I saw that there is nothing better for people than to be
happy in their work. That is why they are here!*
Ecclesiastes 3:22

Many years ago I made notes from a fine business book by Mike Murdock. He listed several keys to achieving happiness in your job. I've adapted a few of these below, and I hope you find them as helpful as I do.

1. Accept work as God's gift, not punishment. Ecclesiastes tells us to rejoice in our work!

2. Recognize God as your true employer. Work with enthusiasm as though you were working for the Lord rather than for people.

3. Be alert to areas in your business that are compatible with your abilities and gifts. If you work hard, there will be progress.

4. Learn everything you can about your job. Read about your field. Take advantage of training. Learn from those who are above you.

5. Establish deadlines and stick to them. Do one thing, finish it, and then move on!

6. Be honest about your mistakes. Don't cover them up.

7. Do more than is expected! Be able to say that you finished the job and it was good.

Making It Personal

Which of these keys do I need to begin implementing?

Asking for Help

So encourage each other and build each other up,
just as you are already doing.
1 Thessalonians 5:11

Back when Premier Designs was a young company, I had some necessary surgery on my right hand. I had to wear a cast for many weeks, and I didn't do too well with my left hand, putting on my earrings and buttoning my jacket. I have always been very independent, and I was embarrassed to feel so helpless.

One day my good friend Maggie said to me, "Why don't you let me help you? This is surely a time you can't do it alone." Well, that did it! I began to realize that God had sent a friend to help when I couldn't get along by myself.

When I remember that incident, I think about how God has always been there for me through other people. I have so many friends who are waiting to give me assistance if I need help. But I need to ask, because they will not force themselves on me.

Our Heavenly Father is waiting to help us, too. But He will not force us to take His help. He loves us with an everlasting love, and He is waiting for us to see our need and seek Him.

Making It Personal

Is it hard for me to ask God, and others, for help? Why?

Time for Thanks

Enter his gates with thanksgiving; go into his courts with praise.
Give thanks to him and bless his name.
Psalm 100:4

This is the time of year when we think about our blessings—blessings that we have received as a nation, as a community, as a family, as a business, and as individuals. Images from our history books of the first Thanksgiving are etched in our minds. The pilgrims were thankful for surviving the hardships of the first year in the new world—the weather, illnesses, and loneliness. They were very public in their thanks to God. Perhaps we also can be more public with our thanksgiving.

Every one of us has the freedom to thank God for His blessings. One of the things I am thankful for is that our beloved country is free, especially when I see others around the world who don't have that same freedom. I am very thankful for my family. God is so good to give us our families, isn't He?

Psalm 100 reminds us to always be thankful: "Give thanks to him and bless his name." Will you take time to reflect on things that you are thankful for?

Making It Personal

How would having an attitude of thanksgiving affect how I live?

Giving Thanks

Praise the LORD, O my soul, and forget not all his benefits.
Psalm 103:2 (NIV)

In 1863, President Abraham Lincoln made the first Thanksgiving Proclamation:

> *I do therefore invite my fellow citizens in every part of the United States, and also those who are at sea and those who are sojourning in foreign lands, to set apart and observe the last Thursday of November next, as a day of Thanksgiving and Praise to our beneficent Father who dwelleth in the Heavens.*

Lincoln went on to urge citizens to take care of the hurting and to fervently implore God to heal the wounds of the nation during the Civil War.

Thanksgiving Day is to be set apart as a day of praise to God. How far we have strayed from its original purpose! Do you ever hear a television host or radio announcer quoting the Thanksgiving Proclamation? Unfortunately, the answer is no! Thanksgiving has come to mean family, football, and feasting. We call it "Turkey Day" and schedule our activities around the big game on television.

Abraham Lincoln invited Americans to give thanks to God, who has given us so much. It is a good thing to give thanks to Him—on Thanksgiving Day and throughout the year.

Making It Personal

How would Thanksgiving be different if we set it apart for giving thanks?

Time for Something New

Throw off your old evil nature and your former way of life,
which is rotten through and through . . . Instead, there
must be a spiritual renewal of your thoughts and attitudes.
Ephesians 4:22-23

A local community play included a big Thanksgiving dinner, complete with a real turkey, roasted to a golden brown. As the play was performed night after night, that poor turkey began to show signs of severe decay. After a couple of weeks, one of the actors said with great deliberation, "I think it's time for a new turkey!"

Are there some "old turkeys" in your life that need to be thrown out? You know, those old habits you can't shake, old sins you can't stop. In the play, the deterioration of the turkey into a discolored, wrinkled leftover was so gradual that no one really noticed until it was beyond salvaging. So it is in our lives. The change in our own attitudes can be so gradual that we may not even notice its effect until the damage is done.

The Bible tells us to throw off our old, sinful nature. Put all those nasty thoughts, old hurts, white lies, petty resentments, mean words, and bad attitudes in a trash bag and toss it—by asking God's forgiveness. Then replace that old stuff with new thoughts and attitudes, with God's help.

Making It Personal

What "old turkeys" in my life need to be thrown out
and replaced with something better?

Faithful Work

*By his faith [Noah] condemned the rest of the world
and was made right in God's sight.*
Hebrews 11:7

One of the most interesting characters in the Bible is a man who was probably the laughingstock of his entire neighborhood. In an area where there was no large body of water, and certainly very little rain, Noah built a boat. But Noah was faithful to the word of God. Hebrews 11:7 tells us, "By his faith he condemned the rest of the world and was made right in God's sight."

Noah certainly acted in a way counter to our culture today. Society tells us we should do what we want to do. Faithfulness says, "You can count on me. I will never let you down." Faithfulness is really born out of faith. And faith is not only believing God can, but that God will.

A wonderful way to find joy in your work is to be faithful. Be faithful to your company and what it stands for. Be faithful to those who believed in you enough to offer you the opportunity to join the company. Be faithful to your family by showing them the value of hard work and the joy reaped from your labor. Be faithful to your employees by being an example to them and showing them the value of consistency.

Making It Personal

*In what ways do I need to go against my culture
in order to be faithful to God?*

The Value of Work

God created the heavens and the earth.
Genesis 1:1

Chuck Colson wrote a valuable book called *Why America Doesn't Work*. The title itself really grabs me because I am an American and I spend many, many hours a week working! And, of course, I'm not alone. Most of us spend about half of our waking life working. We are sometimes even defined by our work. "So what do you do?" is usually the first question we ask when meeting someone for the first time.

The Bible opens with a verse about work. In Genesis 1:1 we read, "God created the heavens and the earth." God created the world, and people in His image. We are to be co-workers with Him.

Work is very important because it provides a sense of accomplishment that is essential for self-esteem. Work is not punishment; it is God's gift. And I, for one, am happy about that, because I love to work—all except the ironing!

Making It Personal

How is work God's gift to me?

November 29

Learning from Critics

If you accept criticism, you will be honored.
Proverbs 13:18

It's easy to shy away from criticism. Listening to someone tell you how you could do something better is very difficult. But one of the ways to find greater joy in your work and relationships is to use criticism to your advantage.

Proverbs 13:18 has a great word about this: "If you ignore criticism, you will end in poverty and disgrace; if you accept criticism, you will be honored." That's pretty straightforward advice. Why is it so hard to take? Maybe because we all think pretty highly of ourselves. We've got our pride, right? We know what we're doing. But that way of thinking is often just a set up for a fall.

So get rid of the pride and get on the positive side of constructive criticism. Seek it out! Go ahead and ask for suggestions in your work. Share ideas with colleagues. Learn what you can from your mistakes when others point them out to you. You'll be amazed how much you will grow.

Making It Personal

How do I usually respond to criticism?

A Good Attitude

Work with enthusiasm, as though you were working for the Lord rather than for people.
Ephesians 6:7

What's one of the best ways to reflect a positive attitude about your work? Smile! Working with a smile shows a good attitude to everyone around you.

Ephesians 6:7 tells us, "Work with enthusiasm, as though you were working for the Lord rather than for people." That is a very good reminder to work with eagerness and joy—with a smile! If we do this, we are sure to please not only the Lord, but we will please others too.

At one of our national rallies, Andy gave us a live demonstration of a big "smile." He came out on stage with a large burlap bag on his back. If you looked closely, the bag had printed on it in large letters: TROUBLES. As Andy sang the song "Pack up your troubles in an old kit bag and smile, smile, smile!" we all began to smile too.

Pack up your troubles for a little while today. Even in the midst of stressful situations, remember to smile. It will bring joy to your heart.

Making It Personal

How can I remember to smile more today?

December

God's great gift to humankind
was motivated by one thing:
love. Merry Christmas!

With love,
Joan

Plenty to Give

The godly love to give!
Proverbs 21:26

God gave us the greatest gift of love: His Son, Jesus. What do we have to give? Here are some things we can give in love:

1. *Time*: This is one of the greatest gifts we can give someone. We must be sensitive to those who need our time and attention, including our families and our colleagues.

2. *Ourselves*: This is an extension of our time, but it is even more practical. We get more out of what we have poured our whole selves into.

3. *Encouragement*: We all experience times of discouragement and need to hear an uplifting word. Be alert to those around you who might need a word of hope.

4. *Compliments*: This is truly a gift to be cherished. Proverbs 25:11 (NKJV) tells us, "A word fitly spoken is like apples of gold in settings of silver."

5. *Money*: Ask God to point out needs—large or small—that you can help meet.

As you can see, we truly have plenty to give away!

Making It Personal

Of the five areas above, which area is hardest for me to give? Why?

Strength for Service

*For I can do everything with the help of Christ
who gives me the strength I need.*
Philippians 4:13

I talk about serving others a lot, and that's on purpose. I don't want to leave the impression that service is something you and I do just because we're such great people. No, service is only service in the highest sense when we do it in love and out of a right relationship with God.

The Lord needs our receptive heart. We need to make ourselves available for Him to use us. And as we do so, we will have the right motive for giving within the context of work or elsewhere.

We may want to serve others. We may want to help others enrich their lives. And we may be able to accomplish good things to some extent. But if we serve in our own energy, we will burn out and not be fulfilled in our business. Why? Because if we are not putting the Lord first, He will not be in our efforts.

It all starts with God. Serving others and enriching their lives happen when we know the Lord and love people with His love.

Making It Personal

Why am I serving? How am I serving?

Keep Hoping

If you are asked about your Christian hope, always be ready to explain it.
1 Peter 3:15

What did you hope to accomplish this year? Maybe you have set goals but have been disappointed when your hopes have not been realized or have been delayed. But God is faithful. Keep hoping. Keep dreaming.

We cannot live without hope. Human hope is essential to physical well-being. Emotional hope means having peace of mind. And spiritual hope means being at peace with God.

When Warden Burl Cain began his work at Angola Prison, the largest maximum-security prison in the United States, he desired two things. First, he wanted to give the inmates a sense of dignity as human beings. Second, he wanted to give them hope—eternal hope and peace with God.

Whether we live and work in Texas, New York, South America, or Angola Prison, we need hope. And we are called to give that hope to others wherever God puts us. There are many ways to spread hope to the hopeless. We have hope in the Lord Jesus Christ! Let's offer hope to others that they might have eternal life and joy unspeakable.

Making It Personal

What role does hope have in my life and work?

December 4

Pray for More

[Jabez] prayed to the God of Israel, "Oh, that you would bless me and extend my lands! Please be with me in all that I do, and keep me from all trouble and pain!" And God granted him his request.

1 Chronicles 4:10

Tucked away in the Old Testament is an interesting notation about a man named Jabez. We don't know much about him except that he was more distinguished than any of his brothers and that he prayed boldly.

His request? That God would: (1) bless him; (2) extend his lands; (3) be with him; and (4) keep him from trouble and pain. Pretty bold prayer! And the Bible says simply, "God granted him his request."

We all need to be more like Jabez, don't we? He didn't say, "Give me a comfortable place where I can retire and look at the beach." No, he looked to God for larger borders, more blessing, more responsibility, and the physical strength he needed to handle it all. He wanted to be stretched. I believe we should desire that, too. What a great example. Have you asked God lately to bless you and enlarge your vision so you will be stretched and grow?

Making It Personal

What keeps me from boldly asking God for His blessing on my life and my business?

The Buck Stops Here

If God has given you leadership ability, take the responsibility seriously.
Romans 12:8

Stanley Marcus, of the Neiman Marcus stores in Dallas, was a much-loved fixture in the retail world of fashion. I love his viewpoints on life. Let me quote from something he said about responsibility:

> *Harry S. Truman had a sign on his desk, which became famous. It said, "The buck stops here!" It was a reminder that, as president, his was the ultimate responsibility… That is both the burden and the privilege of leadership. The person in charge accepts the praise or blame.*

If you are a leader, the buck stops with you. You set the tone. You motivate by example. If you're not careful how you act, you can't expect the leaders under you to follow in an acceptable manner. Don't be afraid to accept responsibility for your actions and your business. You will grow stronger through it.

Making It Personal

Do I accept responsibility or do I tend to pass the buck?

Get Wise

Getting wisdom is the most important thing you can do!
Proverbs 4:7

The book of Proverbs says that wisdom can be acquired through diligent search and obedience to God. Similarly, James 1:5 tells us that if we ask God for wisdom, He will give it. So what do you think—can you have wisdom? Yes, you can. Here are some of the kinds of wisdom you can have:

- Wisdom to do things you've never done before. You can stop looking at the past and start looking at where you are going.
- Wisdom to stay away from negative people. Some people suffer from B.O.; others suffer from B.A.— bad attitude.
- Wisdom to know what decisions will make you a "long termer." You can create your future instead of just thinking about your present. Patience is powerful and productive.
- Wisdom to know your own limitations. For example, you are not wise if you do the work of five or six others by yourself.

If you would like to have this kind of wisdom, ask God for it. Wisdom can be learned.

Making It Personal

What kinds of wisdom will I seek, and how?

A True Compliment

In the end, people appreciate frankness more than flattery.
Proverbs 28:23

A top door-to-door salesman was asked, "To what do you owe your success?"

He replied, "The first five words I say when a woman opens the door are, 'Ma'am, is your mother in?'"

The difference between that kind of fake compliment and a genuine compliment is the motivation behind the words. Ask yourself, "Why am I complimenting this person? Is it truly a gift I desire to give to that person?" If your words are meant as a gift, then that is a compliment.

But we've all received compliments that didn't sound real. Psalm 5:9 tells us we cannot trust a flatterer's words. Flatterers speak only to gain favor, to get attention, or to manipulate someone else.

Ephesians 4:15 refers to speaking "the truth in love," and Proverbs 3:3 says, "Never let loyalty and kindness get away from you." So you see, a compliment is the truth spoken in kindness. And that's a wonderful gift to give and to receive!

Making It Personal

Who can I genuinely compliment today?

December 8

Encouragement That Fits

Worry weighs a person down; an encouraging word cheers a person up.
Proverbs 12:25

As a patient was wheeled into the operating room for major surgery, he was filled with fear and panic when he heard a nurse singing softly the words to the hymn, "Nearer My God to Thee." Wrong timing! It was a perfect time for encouragement, but the nurse wasn't alert to the patient's needs. The words could have been chosen a little more compassionately.

Words of encouragement and praise don't always come naturally, but we can all work on it. We need to fine-tune that gift—and to look on it as a gift, not just a habit.

If you need help with this, why not make a list of people whom God brings to your mind who might need encouragement. Maybe it's a family member, a supervisor, or a neighbor. I guarantee you that a word of encouragement will brighten their day.

I know that sometimes encouraging others is a real challenge. It's almost as if some people don't want you to encourage them. Give those people encouragement anyway, and do it with a smile! Remember, "Anxious hearts are very heavy but a word of encouragement does wonders" (Proverbs 12:25 TLB).

Making It Personal

Who is on my list today for passing out encouragement?

Dream, Dream, Dream

We told the dreams to a young Hebrew man [Joseph] who was a servant of the captain of the guard. He told us what each of our dreams meant, and everything happened just as he said it would.
Genesis 41:12-13

One of my favorite Bible characters is Joseph. Sold by his own brothers into slavery in Egypt, he was imprisoned there. While in prison, he befriended the Pharoah's demoted baker and cupbearer, and God gave Joseph the ability to interpret their dreams. Two years later, Pharaoh himself had two perplexing dreams. He sent for Joseph, and Joseph's amazing interpretations eventually led to his becoming the ruler of Egypt.

I happen to be married to a man who has had many dreams. Andy hasn't been in prison like Joseph, but he had a vision and a dream that led to the founding of our company and its mission. But it seems that most people I know have stopped dreaming. Never before in America have I sensed so much hopelessness. People seem to have lost that hope of new beginnings.

What are you dreaming about today? What are you hoping for? If your dream is from God, have hope that it will one day be fulfilled! God loves it when we dream His dreams and believe that they will one day come to fruition.

Making It Personal

What is my biggest dream right now?

Do As I Do

Don't copy the behavior and customs of this world, but let God transform you.
Romans 12:2

Our actions have far more power than we realize. Albert Bandura, the eminent researcher, once said, "Modeling is the most far-reaching form of unconscious learning there is."

People will forget most of what you say. They will forget almost nothing of what you do. Whatever your pattern, those under you will tend to imitate what you *do*.

So if you really want to be a positive influence in the lives of others, focus on how you act. Do your daily behaviors reflect your desire to serve others? Do you demonstrate what it means to put others first? Do you act with grace and love even when you think no one else is looking? Be a model and others will follow your lead.

Making It Personal

How can I be a positive model in ordinary ways today?

A Worthy Investment

Children are a gift from the LORD.
Psalm 127:3

The longer we are with a company, it seems, the more there is to do. More paperwork, more meetings, more phone calls, more, more, more—and much less time to be with the family. Suddenly, you begin to realize that your children are wondering if you care about them. Those warm chocolate chip cookies after school have disappeared. And when did you last make their favorite meal?

If you have children, God blessed you with a family for a reason. He is counting on you to invest in their lives. No one can take your place. Are you doing the things that are important to your children? Be sure to keep close tabs on their schedule. Be involved in their lives. Work the sports events, dancing lessons, and piano recitals into your schedule.

You must never let your children think you have less interest in their lives just because you have found an exciting career. Spend as much quality time with them as you can. Your investment will be well worth it.

Making It Personal

What's one practical thing I can do to be more involved in my children's lives?

December 12

The Pruning Shears

[The Father] cuts off every branch that doesn't produce fruit, and he prunes the branches that do bear fruit so they will produce even more.

John 15:2

Just as a good gardener inspects his garden, so does my heavenly Father inspect my life. That is a sobering thought to me. Will He find me faithful? Am I making a positive difference in the lives I touch?

I want to live a life that is pleasing to God. I want to be the kind of woman who will bring honor to Him. I believe that is your desire, too. Thankfully, God is at work helping us to fulfill this worthy desire.

If we think about our lives as "gardens," we must remember that in the gardening process there is much weeding and pruning needed. Indeed, you and I need to be constantly pruned by the Lord. As the apostle Paul promised, "God is working in you, giving you the desire to obey him and the power to do what pleases him" (Philippians 2:13).

Scripture also says, "The way to identify a tree or a person is by the kind of fruit that is produced" (Matthew 7:20). We can have a good harvest as God cuts away the unfruitful, dead stuff and leaves the fruitful vines to grow.

Making It Personal

What does God need to prune away in me?

Work Is a Gift

To enjoy your work and accept your lot in life—
that is indeed a gift from God.
Ecclesiastes 5:19

Work began in the Garden of Eden. Adam was to tend to the garden and keep it. This activity provided Adam with a sense of achievement and self-worth. But Adam changed all that. His sin of disobedience turned work into a curse (Genesis 3:19).

Then in Deuteronomy 28, we read that obedience to the laws of God changed all that again, and the blessings of work became the gift of God.

Do you think about work as a gift? You might be motivated by other factors: money, time away from the house, a way to help others. But work is still, above all, a gift from God. Ecclesiastes 5:19-20 tells us we are to rejoice in work. Your work can be a source of joy!

Making It Personal

How can I make my work more joy-filled today?

A Thankful Lifestyle

*No matter what happens, always be thankful, for this
is God's will for you who belong to Christ Jesus.*
1 Thessalonians 5:17-18

I would do almost anything for a person who has proper manners and a thankful heart. I receive many letters of thanks from many people. They don't have to do that, but I love to read their thank-yous. It is polite and kind, and tells me a lot about that person.

In Galatians 5:22, there is a list of Christian characteristics known as the "fruit of the Spirit"—love, joy, peace, patience, kindness, goodness, faithfulness, gentleness and self-control. If we are controlled by God's Holy Spirit, then these qualities will be produced in our lives. But notice that "being thankful" is not on this list. Evidently, that means that being thankful is a choice. We can choose to be thankful or not. The Bible tells us to always be thankful for everything. It is God's will!

How can we do that? Try these ideas: (1) Each morning, write down five things for which you are thankful. (2) Call someone and tell her or him how thankful you are for their friendship. (3) Write a note of thanks to a friend, a family member, a pastor. Make being thankful a lifestyle.

Making It Personal

What can I do today to show my thankfulness?

Life Purpose

Whatever you eat or drink or whatever you do,
you must do all for the glory of God.
1 Corinthians 10:31

Have you ever shaved with a lawn mower, or cut the grass with a razor? Ever brushed your teeth with a comb, or brushed your hair with a toothbrush? No . . . everything has a purpose and is most effective when used for that specific purpose.

Human beings are also made for a purpose—to bring glory to God. While we are serving and enriching lives, I am sure God is well pleased. But our purpose ultimately is to glorify God, to honor Him.

I ask myself often, "What is my purpose in life?" and the answer comes back loud and clear. Jeremiah 29:11 (NIV): "For I know the plans I have for you, Joan, plans to prosper you and not harm you, plans to give you hope and a future." My purpose is to fit in with God's plans for me, which ultimately will bring glory to Him. Those plans have taken me on a journey I could never have predicted. But because it is God's direction, I am purpose-driven and totally fulfilled.

It is an exciting journey when you are doing what God leads you to do. May I never forget my ultimate purpose is to honor God.

Making It Personal

What is my purpose in life?

Taking Responsibility

I plead with you to be of one mind, united in thought and purpose.
1 Corinthians 1:10

When a team like the New York Yankees wins the World Series, there are many people who never set foot on the field as players and yet still share in the rewards. The manager, the coaches, and the trainers, for instance, are all part of the team, too. It's the same with your team. If you are a leader of any kind, you are responsible for your whole team. What, exactly, are your responsibilities as a leader?

1. You are responsible to achieve *unity* among your team members. Start a contest where the most unlikely person can be a winner. Include each team member at your training meetings. Do whatever it takes to make each of them feel like they belong.

2. You are responsible for emphasizing *ethics and professionalism*. Explain your business code of ethics and policies. Encourage them to dress and act professionally at company functions.

3. You are responsible for the *culture* of your group. Keep the personal touch. Keep your promises and do what you say you will do.

Making It Personal

What can I do to show that I value everyone I work with?

The Top Sheep

*Many who are first now will be last then; and
those who are last now will be first then.*
Matthew 20:16

In every animal society, there is an established order of
status within the group. With chickens, it is the pecking
order. With cattle, it is the horning order. Among sheep,
what generally happens is that an arrogant, domineering
old ram butts in and drives the lambs away from their
favorite grazing grounds. Because of the friction, there is
no contentment within the flock.

This is a graphic picture of the struggle for status in
human society. We are always trying not to just keep up
with the Joneses, but to be better than the Joneses, aren't
we? In business, this tendency manifests itself as struggling
for self-recognition, fighting to be the "top sheep," butting
in where we don't belong. In the process, people are hurt.

Jesus taught a better way. He urges us to stop pushing
others down so we can be the top sheep, and learn the way
of humility. Putting others before ourselves is the way of
real blessing.

Making It Personal

*Am I always trying to horn in, dominate,
and be first, no matter who I hurt?*

Given in Love

Then a poor widow came and dropped in two pennies.
Mark 12:42

One well-known story in the Bible is that of the widow who gave two pennies to the temple coffers. Jesus said, "I assure you, this poor widow has given more than all the others have given. For they gave a tiny part of their surplus, but she, poor as she is, has given everything she has" (Mark 12:43-44).

A penny is the smallest coin we have. It's just a little thing. But suppose I need help in my business. You offer to help me. I tell you that I will pay you a penny the first day you help me, double that the second day, double that amount the third day, and so on until the end of the month. Would you take the job for those wages? If I hired you on that basis, I would owe you over $5 million dollars on the last day of the month! I doubt even the richest man in all the world could afford to hire you on that basis.

You see, a very small thing can multiply fast. This is true of giving as well. Giving is usually just that little thing: the compliment, the time we spend, the encouragement we give. A small thing given in love will multiply and multiply!

Making It Personal

How have I seen a small gift multiply in my life?

December 19

The Joy of the Lord

The joy of the LORD is your strength!
Nehemiah 8:10

Isaac Watts wrote the words to the popular Christmas carol "Joy to the World." Why proclaim joy? Because the Lord of peace and joy has come!

Peace and joy will not happen in any permanent way in a heart until a person accepts Christ and makes Him Lord of their life. When the apostle Paul wrote Philippians, he was in jail and facing hard times. He had been abandoned by friends and coworkers, yet he was still able to say, "Always be full of joy in the Lord" (Philippians 4:4).

Joy is a byproduct of a relationship with God, not something you work to get. You know when you have it, but you rarely sense where it came from or how you got it. Happiness passes, but joy abides. Joy is gladness of heart, an inner feeling that is expressed outwardly.

Today, may God give you joy in your heart, a smile on your face, and a lift in your walk.

Making It Personal

Do I feel joy in my heart? Can others see it on my face?

December 20

Dark Days of Winter

*As long as the earth remains, there will be springtime and harvest,
cold and heat, winter and summer, day and night.*
Genesis 8:22

I am not a winter person; I prefer sunshine and warmth! To me, winter is cold and dreary, with its lack of color, frozen lakes, bare tree limbs, short days and long nights. The only hope is that spring is coming.

That's the message we must remember in the wintertime—hope will emerge! Good things will come again. Maybe your fall season was full of life and joy, but suddenly you seem to be "on hold." Or maybe you are in a dry winter season and you feel alone. Whatever the situation, you can reach out to others and do good things to help them. And always remember that spring will come again.

Sometimes in the dark days of winter, it helps lift our spirits to remember what God has promised. One of my favorite Scripture verses is Psalm 115:3, "Our God is in the heavens, and he does as he wishes." God is in control!

Making It Personal

How do I handle the "winter" seasons in my life?

Tree of Giving

*But God showed his great love for us by sending Christ
to die for us while we were still sinners.*
Romans 5:8

In a popular folk tale, three little trees dream about what they want to become.

The first tree wanted to become a treasure chest holding great treasure. But eventually it was cut down and made into a crude manger in which a baby was born.

The second little tree wanted to become a great sailing ship and carry great men. Instead it was carved into a simple fishing boat, in which a man sat to teach a crowd.

The third tree dreamed of being the tallest tree so he could point people to God. It was hewn into a splintery, rugged cross upon which a man died.

Little did they know that all their dreams came true! The cradle held the greatest treasure of all: our infant Savior. The boat carried Jesus, the greatest man who ever lived. The cross pointed people to God, and to the real reason for the Christmas season: "For God so loved the world that he gave his only Son, so that everyone who believes in him will not perish but have eternal life" (John 3:16).

Making It Personal

How can I point others to the real reason for the season?

The Perfect Gift

If your gift is that of serving others, serve them well. . . .
If your gift is to encourage others, do it! . . . . And if you have a gift for
showing kindness to others, do it gladly.
Romans 12:7-8

In this Christmas season of gift giving, most of us rush around trying to find the elusive perfect gift. Let me remind you that you already have the ideal gift to give.

You don't have to go to the nearest mall to find it. You don't have to search in a catalog. It is already in your home. It has great value but no sales tag on it. It's never the wrong size. You don't have to assemble any parts. You don't even have to wrap it with fancy wrapping paper.

The perfect gift is *you!*

Christmas is a joyful time for celebrations, but for many people it is a lonely season. There are people all around us who need an encouraging word. So instead of buying things that don't last, try giving something of yourself—a smile, a kind word, a note, a visit. That is truly the gift that keeps on giving.

Making It Personal

What is one creative way I can give of myself this Christmas?

It's Free

For God so loved the world that he gave his only Son.
John 3:16

Have you noticed how gifts keep getting more and more expensive? Retailers gear up earlier every year in anticipation of doing more than 15 percent of their annual business during the Christmas season. We've all heard of the ultra-expensive items in certain catalogs: everything from his-and-hers camels to exotic cruises.

But the world's most costly gift doesn't come from any catalog and has no price tag. It's God's free gift to us—His Son, Jesus.

Christmas is the time we honor and celebrate the birth of Jesus Christ, who was born in a tiny town in Judea more than 2,000 years ago. No fact in history is as well documented as the birth, life, death, and resurrection of Jesus Christ. And God's great gift to humankind was motivated by one thing: *love*. "God so loved the world that he gave his only Son."

Making It Personal

How will I respond to God's free gift of love this Christmas?

The Christmas Flower

*[Mary] will have a son, and you are to name him Jesus,
for he will save his people from their sins.*
Matthew 1:21

A story is told of a young girl in Mexico whose name was Aleta. She knew that others would go to church on Christmas Eve and place flowers and gifts for baby Jesus in the Nativity scene. But she had nothing to show her love for the Christ Child. So she wept.

An angel appeared and told her, "Gather an armful of weeds by the roadside, and when you come to the altar, place them by the crib." Aleta felt uncertain. Nevertheless, she promised to do as the angel said.

Christmas Eve came. The church was beautifully lit and everyone made their way to the service. Aleta came and gently laid her weeds among the lovely flowers, and then bowed her head in adoration.

Suddenly a gasp of delight came from people in the church. To everyone's astonishment, the weeds had become beautiful scarlet flowers! And ever since, these flowers have been known as the poinsettia—the Christmas flower.

Making It Personal

In what small way can I honor Jesus this Christmas season?

Good News!

I bring you good news of great joy for everyone! The Savior—yes, the Messiah, the Lord—has been born tonight in Bethlehem!
Luke 2:10-11

Busyness often prevents us from reflecting on the real reason for Christmas, which commemorates the birth of Christ. Yes, this is a celebration time, a time to be grateful for health, wealth, friends, food, and shelter. But it is more than that. It is also a time to thank our heavenly Father for sending us a gift that cost Him so much and us nothing, a gift that gives us real peace and hope, and that is available to all.

Remember the good news of the angelic message: "The Savior—yes, the Messiah, the Lord—has been born!" Like the shepherds who came and found Jesus, we also can come and find Him, not as a babe in a manger, but as our Savior, who died and rose again, and lives in heaven.

Amid all the activities and your sweet family togetherness, the beautiful spirit of Christmas can be smothered. So this year give yourself a special gift—a few minutes of quiet time for reflecting on God's marvelous gift to us.

Making It Personal

When will I take time to reflect on God's special gift to me?

December 26

Box It Away

Get rid of your evil deeds. Shed them like dirty clothes.
Romans 13:12

Have you ever looked in the dictionary and seen several meanings for a word? It can be quite an education.

Take the word *box*. There are many types of boxes listed: box berry, boxboard, box camera, boxcar, box elder, boxer shorts, and on and on. As I read, I finally found the one I was looking for: "Boxing Day." In England and Canada, the first weekday after Christmas is a legal holiday. In Canada, where I was born, Boxing Day was a busy day. We unpacked all the Christmas gifts from their boxes, and then put all the boxes out in the trash, never to be used again.

I think this Boxing Day is a good time to make a list of things we might like to add to that pile of boxes headed for the trash: impatience, rudeness, laziness, unbalanced lifestyles, half-truths, unforgiveness, anger, bad habits. There are "boxes" everywhere! Make your own list and observe a Boxing Day in your home this year.

Making It Personal

What negative things in my life do I need to box up and get rid of?

The Power of One

He existed before everything else began, and he holds all creation together.
Colossians 1:17

I once read an article that asked, "Can you imagine what this world would be like if Jesus Christ had never been born?" Take some time to think about that.

Imagine living in a world with no Christian values, no Bible, no prayer, no churches. Much of the wisdom and knowledge that permeates our society, and much of the comforts that we enjoy as Americans are a result of our nation being founded on Christian principles and values. Many of the hospitals, social services, and higher education institutions around the world were begun by Christ-followers. It's hard to deny the power and effect of that one man who lived over two thousand years ago.

But Jesus was no ordinary man; He was God. And He came in order that we might have life now and life eternal. Real joy and peace comes when we know Him personally and serve Him daily.

Making It Personal

How does the fact of Christ's birth influence my culture and community?

Attention to Detail

*The LORD says, "I will guide you along the best pathway for your life.
I will advise you and watch over you."*
Psalm 32:8 (Verse of the Year 1997)

It has been said the difference between something good and something great is attention to detail. When Andy and I started our business, we paid attention to the details and did what was right. We have stayed the course, maintaining the original Philosophy, Purpose, and Plan as we watched our dream unfold into reality. So we're set, right? Not exactly. If we forget to follow the details of those core values, we'll be going down the wrong path.

King Solomon had an annual income of millions, ruled over a vast kingdom, and was wiser than all the kings of earth. He had it all. He was set, right? Not exactly. Things slowly began to change. A little compromise here, a little disobedience there. Solomon did not pay attention to the details God had commanded him to follow. He drifted from the path so much that at the end of his life he was going in an entirely different direction.

Be careful with every new step in life that you take. Stay on God's course for you; don't stray from it, so you can say with the psalmist, "My steps have stayed on your path; I have not wavered from following you" (Psalm 17:5).

Making It Personal

*Am I straying from the right path for my life?
What adjustments do I need to make?*

Waste No Time

Why do the people waste their time with futile plans?
Psalm 2:1

Time is a precious commodity. We often say, "I just don't know where the time went!" or "Time just got away from me." Yet each of us is allotted 168 hours per week, no more and no less than anyone else.

Time is precious. We use it, save it, spend it, waste it, lose it. Time seems like such a small thing, and yet, we reveal so much about ourselves by how we spend our time. Are we careful stewards of what God has entrusted to us?

A new year is beginning, with fresh time to use as we wish. Wipe the slate clean, get rid of negative feelings and baggage from the past. Waste no time in moving into the future with confidence.

Making It Personal

What are some ways I waste time?

Look Forward

*For I can do everything with the help of Christ
who gives me the strength I need.*
Philippians 4:13

Sometimes we get caught up in what we could have done in business in the past. But whatever we could have accomplished or contributed is now history. In spite of all our good intentions and commitments, we've left much undone. The wonderful thing is—today is a new beginning! We can start with a fresh, clean page.

I like the story about the Danish sculptor Bertel Thorvaldsen. He was asked which of his statues was the greatest. He replied, "The next one." That's the way we should feel about our business. Regardless of past failures or accomplishments, we always have the opportunity to do a better job next time.

None of us knows what each new day will bring, but let's remember to:

- Look Back— Thank Him
- Look Around— Serve Him
- Look Forward—Trust Him
- Look Up—Expect Him

Making It Personal

*In what ways do my thoughts about the past
affect how I view the future?*

Out with the Old

Forgetting the past and looking forward to what lies ahead.
Philippians 3:13

In certain parts of Italy the people have a wonderful custom. As midnight approaches on New Year's Eve, the streets clear out. There is no traffic. There are no pedestrians. Even the police officers take cover. Then, at the stroke of midnight, the windows of the houses fly open. To the sound of laughter, music, and fireworks, each member of the family pitches out unwanted stuff. This includes old crockery, broken ornaments, used furniture and personal possessions that remind them of events or feelings in the past year they want to get rid of.

Many of us accumulate all kinds of mental and emotional stuff and bring it with us from the past into the future. But now is a perfect time to sort through and throw some stuff out the window. Go through the closets, drawers, and attics of your life and toss out all the trash. I'm talking about hurts and disappointments, goals you didn't meet, unhappy customers, unwarranted criticism, unkind words, stubborn attitudes, dumb mistakes, bad habits, and the like. Get rid of whatever will hold you back in this new year.

Making It Personal

What old stuff in my life do I need to heave out the window to start this year fresh?